Workshop Models for Family Life Education

Overcoming Relationship Addiction

A Workshop for Women Who Love Too Much

Workshop Models for Family Life Education

Overcoming Relationship Addiction

A Workshop for Women Who Love Too Much

Kathryn Apgar

FSA Family Service America
Milwaukee, Wisconsin

Family Service America
11700 West Lake Park Drive
Milwaukee, Wisconsin 53224

Library of Congress Cataloging-in-Publication Data

Apgar, Kathryn.
Relationship addiction : a workshop for women who love too much / Kathryn Apgar.
p. cm. — (Workshop models for family life education)
ISBN 0-87304-239-5
1. Relationship addiction—Treatment. 2. Group psychotherapy. 3. Women—Mental health. 4. Love—Psychological aspects. I. Title. II. Series.
RC552.R44A64 1990
616.86–dc20 90–39462

Printed in the United States

Table of Contents

Preface

Workshop Models for Family Life Education is a series of manuals intended to promote the exploration of new alternatives and the utilization of new options in day-to-day living through programs in family life education.

Basically, family life education (FLE) is a service of planned intervention that applies the dynamic process of group learning to improving the quality of individual and family living. The manuals are in workshop format and offer new approaches to service to families. They are meant to serve as a training mechanism and basic framework for group leaders involved in FLE workshops.

In 1974, the Family Service Association of America (FSAA), now Family Service America, appointed a National Task Force on Family Life Education, Development, and Enrichment. One of the goals of the task force was to assess the importance and future direction of FLE services within family service agencies. One of the recommendations of its report was to "recognize family life education, development, and enrichment as one of the three major services of the family service agency: family counseling, family life education, and family advocacy."[1] This recommendation was adopted by the association's Board of Directors and has become basic policy.

An interest in FLE is a natural development of Family Service America's role in the strengthening of family life and complementary to the more traditional remedial functions of family agencies. Family Life Education programs can add a new dimension to the services provided by family agencies. They can open an agency to the general population by providing programs that are appropriate for all families and individuals, not only for those at risk. They provide a new arena for service that deals with growth as well as dysfunction. They can encourage agencies to look beyond the therapeutic approach and to take on a new objective for the enrichment and strengthening of family life. For the participants, FLE programs can lead to increased understanding of normal stress, growth of esteem for one's self and others, development of communications skills, improved ability to cope with problem situations, development of problem-solving skills, and maximization of family and individual potential.

This series provides tangible evidence of Family Service America's continuing interest in FLE and of a belief in its future importance for family services. Family Life Education programs, coordinated within a total agency program and viewed as a vital and integral part of the agency, can become key factors in promoting growth and development within all families.

1. "Overview of Findings of the FSAA Task Force on Family Life Education, Development, and Enrichment," mimeographed (New York: Family Service Association of America, May 1976), p. 21.

Introduction

Family Service of Greater Boston, Boston, Massachusetts, offers a number of family life enrichment programs for individuals and families. The workshop program presented here is designed for women who are involved in or who tend to become habitually involved in dysfunctional, addictive relationships with men. The workshop draws extensively from the work of Robin Norwood's *Women Who Love Too Much*, translating many of the concepts in her best-selling book into a workshop format that can be used by family life education professionals to initiate and conduct workshops for women involved in addictive relationships.

At a time when men, women, and children are forced by societal circumstances to structure and organize their lives in order to survive cultural, family, work, and social pressures, women are more interested than ever before in healthy and constructive relationships. Women are no longer willing to drift along in an unhealthy relationship just because "that's the way it always has been." But a changing culture does not necessarily alter the long-standing habits developed in childhood. Women who are involved in or who habitually become involved in destructive relationships need to investigate the dynamics of their past and current relationships if they are to develop healthy, sharing relationships with their partners. They must confront issues of trust, anger, expression of feelings, and self-esteem before they can change the dynamics of their relationships. In other words, to change their relationships, they must change themselves. This workshop model is designed to help family life enrichment professionals help their clients make these changes in their lives.

The six-session workshop model provides a structured and supportive group environment in which women can confront and deal with these issues. The group format helps dispel women's sense of isolation and to discover the impact of their childhood relationships on their present relationships. The group format provides support and positive feedback to members, allowing them to share their experiences and feelings. By learning how to identify with, relate to, and share with one another, members learn how to develop and sustain constructive personal relationships outside their relationship with their partner. In a word, they learn to value and trust themselves, the necessary first step in developing healthy relationships with anyone, male or female.

WORKSHOP FORMAT

The workshop consists of six two-hour sessions. The workshop is most effective when membership is limited to fifteen participants. Workshops with ten to twelve participants are most effective, allowing more time for individual sharing and group discussion. Mini-lectures provide didactic information to the participants. In addition, numerous exercises are conducted in small groups, with opportunities to discuss with the larger group what members have experienced and learned.

Because the sharing of feelings is encouraged, group leaders must be extremely sensitive to what is occurring among individuals and within the group. The group leader must offer support and validation and encourage group members to do the same. It is important to remember that the workshop is *not* therapy or group treatment. The workshop is designed to help women involved in dysfunctional personal relationships to learn how to help themselves. The focus is on education, not therapy.

Group leaders must have in-depth knowledge and understanding of relationship addiction in particular and co-dependency issues in general. Leaders must be prepared to answer questions concerning relationship addiction and to facilitate supportive relationships among group members. They must also be able to admit their lack of knowledge, and willingness to find an answer, when circumstances demand. Group leaders should be familiar with the literature on relationship addiction. (See the Suggested Reading List in the handout section at the end of Session 1.)

Leaders should familiarize themselves thoroughly with the manual before beginning the workshop. They should review the material for each session before presenting it in the workshop. It is important that leaders be able to discuss the material with participants and not present it in a lecture format.

Arranging chairs in a circle before members arrive saves time and facilitates sharing. Transferring visual materials to a flip chart should also be done in advance. Flip charts are important teaching tools in that they help the leader emphasize and reinforce important points.

Sessions should be presented in the order given, because the themes and issues have been organized to lead group members step by step through their relationship issues. However, the material can be adapted to individual group needs. For example, as group members become comfortable with the group, discussion may increase and leaders may find it difficult to cover all the material in a given session. Pacing and timing of material will depend on the particular group as well as the leader's experience and familiarity with the material, but in general group leaders may have to fit mini-lectures into the group discussions. Or the leaders may want to divide the workshop material into eight sessions instead of six.

Obviously, the most important thing for group leaders to remember is to remain sensitive to the feelings and experiences of group members. Although the workshop sessions are highly structured, they can (and should) be adapted to meet the needs of the group and the style of the leader. In developing her relationship with the group, the leader is providing an important model that participants can use with their own relationships.

Preparation for the Workshop

RECRUITING FOR THE GROUP

Combining several approaches should result in successful recruiting for the workshop.

For group leaders who are associated with or in practice at a family service agency, mental health clinic, or other treatment facility, recruitment can begin with one's own clients. Clients should be made aware of the benefits of the group experience and told that it is designed to address their specific needs and issues. Leaders should educate and inform other agency staff about whom the workshop would benefit so that appropriate client referrals can be made.

Public service radio announcements, either thirty or sixty seconds long, help generate inquiries and client registration. Newspapers will also run a feature article on a workshop or announce the starting date of the new program under their listing of community events.

REGISTRATION

Registration can begin on the telephone. When potential clients call to inquire about the group, they should be told that the workshop is not a therapy group or self-help program but an adult education workshop with an experiential component. The leader should give a broad overview of the content of each session, as well as information about the time, dates, and fee for the workshop. Some individuals may be hesitant to commit for the full workshop because of their anxiety about confronting personal issues. However, potential registrants should be told that they should register only if they are willing to make a commitment for the full workshop, barring illness or unforeseen events. Members should be told to arrive fifteen to twenty minutes before the first group meeting to pay the registration fee for the workshop and to complete the paperwork.

The use of name tags is a good idea for at least the first few group sessions and may facilitate sharing in small groups. Groups should meet in a room that comfortably accommodates the size of the group. Chairs should be placed in an open circle, with the leader's chair and flip chart at the open end.

SESSION 1
Love Addiction—Defined

OBJECTIVES:

To make participants feel comfortable in the workshop.
To provide general information on workshop objectives.
To establish guidelines for meetings.
To define love addiction.

I. INTRODUCTION

A. As group members enter the room, give them "Workshop Objectives," "Guidelines for Meetings," and "Suggested Readings" (see Session 1 handouts).

B. Introduction of Leader
When group members are seated, the leader introduces herself to the group by giving her name, position or title, and other appropriate information. Providing information on professional background helps establish confidence in the leader among participants.

C. Purpose of Workshop
The group leader may wish to state the following: Welcome to the first meeting of Women Who Love Too Much. My name is _________, and I'm a woman who often loved too much. I believe that most women say this about themselves at some time in their life.

This workshop is designed for women who wish to explore their pattern of loving too much and to change their style of loving to a healthier way of relating. Many of the concepts and ideas in this workshop are drawn from Robin Norwood's best-selling book, *Women Who Love Too Much.*[1] Many other ideas have been added from other books and materials. Many of you have probably already read Robin Norwood's book. How many? Most women feel an instant tug of recognition when they read it. I certainly did. Many of my clients told me about how the stories in the book had personal meaning for them. For some clients, the book helped them change how they think about themselves and how they live.

Loving too much is about *relationship addiction, addiction to a particular relationship*, and *addiction to having a relationship*. As Robin Norwood describes it, when a woman loves too much, when she suffers from addiction to a relationship, "*being in love means being in pain.*"[2]

Loving too much is also experienced by some men, between parents and children, between other family members, between friends, and by gay couples. Women relate this way more commonly, however, because they are socialized to be nurturers and caretakers. Thus they can become stuck in viewing caretaking and nurturing as their only legitimate roles. A woman may take care of the whole world and neglect to take care of herself. When a woman or a man sees nurturing or caretaking as the only way to give and receive love and as the only way to feel worthwhile, then he or she is likely to love too much. In our society, however, this occurs more frequently among women. In some families women learn to take care of others and to deny their own needs for care. If you ask a little girl what she wants to be when she grows up, most likely she'll reply, "A mommy." Little boys want to be astronauts, policemen, or firemen.

From infancy, girls are encouraged to develop a strong interest in relationships, to be sensitive to the feelings of others and their needs. Boys are encouraged to focus on skills and achievements. Adult males often have not learned that relationships are important to their well-being. Recent work has focused on developing a theory of growth and development in women. Researchers have found that women develop an individual identity not through breaking early emotional ties with parents and parent figures, as do males, but through a "process of growth within relationships where both or all people involved are encouraged and challenged to maintain connection and to foster, adapt and change with the growth of the other."[3] This development of "self-in-relationship" helps women validate themselves, but it can also foster the personal growth of others at the expense of self.

A woman in an addictive relationship will preserve the relationship despite costs to her own emotional and physical safety. She is often unable to function adequately in other areas of her life. One woman told me she had lost one job and was about to lose another because of her addictive relationship with her boyfriend.

During the course of this workshop, we'll look at what relationship addiction and loving too much are like, how women experience it, and how women express it. We'll explore some of the reasons a woman will relate to a lover as if she were hooked. We'll consider why women stay in relationships that are unhealthy and painful and sometimes even seek them out, and how wanting to be in a love relationship can itself become an addiction.

The workshop has three major goals:

- To help you gain a clearer understanding of your own relationship addiction patterns.
- To provide you with tools to help you develop relationships that are not addictive.
- To help you obtain support and encouragement from other women in the group who have experienced some of the same pains so that you can work toward changing your pattern of loving too much.

D. Introduction of Members

Ask each participant to introduce herself and state her relationship status: single, married, divorced, separated, living with partner, has boyfriend, number of children and their ages. Participant may be asked to share one quality about herself that shows that she is a woman who loves too much (this statement is voluntary). Ask participants to describe what they expect to gain from the workshop. The leader should model this activity:

"My name is _____. I'm a woman who loves too much because I keep hoping my partner will change—be more fun-loving and playful. I hope this group will help me to stop hoping for what may be impossible to achieve and to put my energy into creating a more enjoyable life for myself."

List participants' workshop expectations on a chart.

II. EXERCISE ONE: SHARING EXPECTATIONS OF GROUP MEMBERS

A. Ask participants to pair up with a group member whom they do not know.

B. Ask members to interview their partner for the purpose of getting acquainted and setting learning goals. Partner should be asked why she decided to attend this group and what she hopes to learn from the workshop.

C. Have group members introduce partner to the group and state what their partner hopes to learn.

D. List any new goals on chart.

III. GUIDELINES FOR MEETINGS

Ask group to review guidelines and encourage questions regarding items they do not understand. Leader may add the following comments:

Because we're not a therapy group, we don't have time to hear each participant's story in depth. Our group may often be larger than a therapy group of six to eight persons. Our purpose is to help you gain an understanding of how women love too much, identify your own pattern of loving too much, to help you discover tools for changing these patterns, and to provide support and ideas from the group.

You may need and want more time for sharing than is available in the group activities. In other words, you may feel that you have unfinished business. Decide how you want to take care of these issues after the session. You may want to telephone one another or get together with one or more people with whom you feel comfortable after the meeting or between meetings.

Each of you will establish your own pace in proceeding toward your goals. Find a pace that feels right for you. You'll need to let go of your wish for an instant solution to your problems. Quick fixes don't happen. The solutions are in yourself—in what you make happen. You should respect your own pace and readiness for change as well as respect the pace and readiness for change of everyone in the group. Give yourself and others in the group recognition for the smallest positive changes in thinking, feeling, and doing. Give yourself a pat on the back for starting a long-term process of change by coming to the group. By attending the group, you've already begun to change how you think about yourself by demonstrating that you do not want negative relationships and that you expect positive, healthy relationships.

IV. LOVE ADDICTION—WHAT IS IT?

Mini-Lecture: Defining Love Addiction
All love relationships have some addictive elements. Our dependency on others isn't always bad. Often it's necessary for survival. But when does dependency become unhealthy, and how can you tell if your love is addictive?

Robin Norwood states, "Loving too much means obsessing about a man and calling that obsession love, allowing it to control your emotions and much of your behavior, realizing that it negatively influences your health and well-being yet finding yourself unable to let go."[4]

The root of the obsession is *fear*, not love—fear of being alone, unlovable, abandoned, ignored, unworthy. To protect ourselves from these fears, we try to manipulate others so they'll take care of us and our problems. We give love in order to get it back. When this doesn't work, we try harder—and end up loving too much.

Brenda Schaeffer says: "Love addiction is our reliance on someone else to get our needs fulfilled, to provide us safety and predictability, to avoid fear or emotional pain, to solve our problems and to keep our balance." She points out that "the paradox is that love addiction represents our attempt to gain control of our lives, but we lose control by giving personal power to someone other than ourselves."[5]

Love addiction creates passivity. We become reactors as opposed to *actors*. We react to someone else's thoughts, feelings, behaviors. We don't take action by making things happen in our own lives. We try to get others to take care of us, often becoming manipulative. Addictive lovers think that by caring for and loving their partner the way they want to be loved, eventually their partner will love them the same way.

In *Love and Addiction*, Stanton Peele and Archie Brodsky describe the addicting element in love relationships as the compelling need the person feels to connect with and to remain connected with a particular person.[6] Although love and commitment may be present in such a relationship, in genuinely loving and committed relationships, both persons are free to choose whether to love. They don't experience a compelling need to do so. When we feel driven by a compulsive need to love, we feel that we have no choice. It's as if we say to ourselves, "I must have this person even if this relationship is bad for me." Additionally, when a woman who loves too much isn't in a relationship, she may feel a compulsive need to have a relationship: "I must have a relationship with a man—any relationship—even if that relationship is not good for me."

Codependency and loving too much share similarities. Charlotte Davis Kasl states, "The co-dependent will be extremely dependent on another person, he or she will try to control the partner too much and seek their identity through others. They pay for care with self-sacrifice. The antidote for co-dependency and loving too much is learning to love yourself."[7]

Howard Halpern identifies indicators of an addictive relationship:

- Compulsive quality in the experience of the relationship
- Feelings of panic when the person is absent and at

the thought of ending the relationship

- Withdrawal symptoms when the relationship ends: pains in chest, stomach, abdomen, crying, sleep disturbances (too little, too much) irritability, depression
- After the mourning period for the ended relationship has passed, feeling liberated, triumphant, sense of accomplishment[8]

Like addiction to a substance, a woman who is addicted to love experiences certain feelings, beliefs, and behaviors (list on blackboard or chart).

Feelings

- Incompleteness
- Emptiness
- Despair
- Sadness
- Being lost

Beliefs

- Belief that the resolution of these feelings lies in connecting oneself to something or someone outside of oneself

Behaviors

- The person becomes the center of one's life
- The addicted person risks her mental or physical health to maintain a relationship
- The addicted person discounts her own accomplishments and strengths, feels that she lacks worth if she's not involved in a relationship
- Feelings of neediness deprive self of essential freedom in relationships—freedom to be her best self, freedom to choose to stay in or quit the relationship, freedom to love through choice and caring

V. EXERCISE TWO: SIGNS OF LOVE ADDICTION IN OURSELVES

A. Distribute "Signs of Addiction" handout.

B. Ask members to do the following with partner:

1. Share what signs you recognize in yourself (present

and/or past relationships).
2. Tell your partner what these experiences were like for you and how you tried to cope.

C. As a group, discuss the following:
1. How many of you recognize yourself in most signs? In two or more signs?
2. What sign stands out for you?
3. What are the commonalities among the signs?

D. Tell group the following: The first step is to recognize that you are hooked and to understand what that means for you. As you begin to understand how the addiction works in your own life, you'll develop a clear idea of what you want to change.

VI. HOME ACTIVITY

A. Distribute the following handouts: "Characteristics of a Woman Who Loves Too Much," "Characteristics of a Woman Recovered from Loving Too Much," and "How Does Your Relationship Rate?"

B. Instruct participants to complete handouts at home prior to the next session.

C. Purpose: To gain a clearer understanding of how you love too much. These handouts will help you prepare for setting goals for change, which will be discussed in Session 2. They will also help you focus on your priorities for growth and change as well as on steps you can take to free yourself from love addiction.

D. Instructions
1. Characteristics of a Woman Who Loves Too Much
   - Check (✔) items that you identify with.
   - Star (✳) items that you are working on.
2. Characteristics of a Woman Recovered from Loving Too Much
   - Check (✔) items that you identify with.
   - Star (✳) items that you are working on or

agree that you will work on.

3. How Does Your Relationship Rate?
   - Score yourself from 0–5 (0 = never; 5 = always) on addictive love and mature love characteristics.

E. Instruct members to bring handouts to Session 2. Ask members if they have any questions.

VII. CLOSING

Group members should be encouraged to give one another continuing support between sessions by calling on the telephone or getting together informally. Suggest to members that they may want to exchange phone numbers now. This can be done as a group, if they all agree. Index cards can be handed out on which members can write down numbers.

Some groups enjoy the following closing ritual: Stand in a circle. Hold hands if you wish. Taking turns, each participant sings out her first name and the group sings it back to her like an echo. The leader should model this ritual.

The group can also be asked to develop their own closing, for example, taking turns each week reading an affirmation of strength for the group, such as a brief verse or a statement to meditate on. *Meditations for Women: Each Day a New Beginning*[9] provides useful meditations. The leader can select appropriate ones for the session and ask someone to read. Or the designated member can select and read the passage.

REFERENCES

1. Robin Norwood, *Women Who Love Too Much* (New York: Pocket Books, 1985).
2. Ibid.
3. Janet Surrey, "Self in Relation: A Theory of Women's Development" (Stone Center, Wellesley College, 1985).
4. Norwood, *Women Who Love Too Much*, p. 5.

5. Brenda Schaeffer, *Is It Love or Is It Addiction?* (Minneapolis: Hazelden, 1987), p. 5.
6. Stanton Peele and Archie Brodsky, *Love and Addiction* (New York: Tapinger, 1975.)
7. Charlotte Davis Kasl, *Women, Sex and Addiction: A Search for Love and Power* (New York: Ticknor and Fields, 1989).
8. Howard Halpern, *How to Break Your Addiction to a Person* (New York: McGraw-Hill, 1982), pp. 7–10.
9. *Meditations for Women: Each Day a New Beginning* (Minneapolis: Hazelden, 1982).

Handout—Session 1

Relationship Addiction: A Workshop for Women Who Love Too Much

General Objectives of the Workshop

- To increase your awareness of the many ways women love too much
- To assess and explore some of the reasons women love too much
- To increase your ability to make better decisions about ways to care for yourself in relationships
- To receive support from the group, which serves as a safe place to explore your pattern of loving too much
- To provide some tools to assist you in changing your style of loving to a more fulfilling way of relating

Workshop Sessions

- **Session 1: Love Addiction—Defined**
    - Introduction
    - Exercise: Sharing Expectations of Group Members
    - Guidelines for Meetings
    - Love Addiction—What Is It?
    - Exercise: Signs of Love Addiction in Ourselves
    - Home Activity
    - Closing
- **Session 2: What We Do**
    - Session 1 Review
    - Review and Discussion of Home Activities
    - Exercise: Goal Setting and Priorities for Growth and Change
    - Exercise: Visualizing Taking That Step
    - Exercise: Sentence Completion
    - Exercise: Being Your Own Best Friend
    - Home Activity
    - Closing

- **Session 3: Why We Do It**
  - Session 2 Review
  - Review and Discussion of Home Activities
  - Affirming Yourself
  - Mastering the Past—The Myth
  - Awareness Exercise—Mr. Nice Guy
  - Home Activities
  - Closing

- **Session 4: Letting Go of Old Relationship Patterns**
  - Session 3 Review
  - Letting Go of Old Roles
  - The Overresponsible Role
  - The Caretaker Role
  - The Superadaptable Role
  - Visualization: Letting Go of Old Roles
  - Responses of Others to Your Changing Role Patterns
  - Closing

- **Session 5: Making Better Decisions**
  - Session 4 Review
  - Relationship Evaluation Inventories
  - What Is a Healthy Relationship?
  - Making Better Decisions
  - Preparation for the Final Session
  - Closing

- **Session 6: Staying Unhooked**
  - Session 5 Review
  - Staying Unhooked
  - Exercises: Thoughts and Feelings, Parenting Your Inner Child, Celebrating Your Empowerment
  - Workshop Evaluations
  - Ongoing Support
  - Closing

Handout—Session 1

Guidelines for Meetings

Guidelines for meetings help establish harmony and cohesion and a sense of common purpose in the group. These guidelines are not rules; they are designed to help develop a successful support system among group members.*

- Participants should not give advice, criticize, interrogate, or pressure another member to speak. Suggesting options or choices is very different from giving advice. Such suggestions are always welcomed (subject to the following guideline).
- Do not provide unsolicited feedback unless feedback is requested by the person sharing personal information or unless permission to do so is requested.
- Debating and arguing with one another does not benefit the group. Remember, we are a support group. Our goal is to be supportive of one another.
- Individuals should avoid dominating or controlling others in the group. Be aware of the length of time you speak and how often you speak. Everyone deserves some time for sharing. Also, no one member knows all the answers; therefore, individuals should not try to control the group or make independent decisions for it.
- Avoid talking too much about *him.* Remember, we are not meeting to gripe about men. Group members must learn to focus on themselves—their own thoughts, feelings, behaviors, and development in recovery.
- Maintain confidentiality. Anonymity promotes trust and a safe place for sharing.
- Controversial subjects or outside issues should not be discussed, so that the primary purpose of the group is not lost.
- If you do not want to respond, just say, "I pass."

*Guidelines are adapted from Robin Norwood, *Women Who Love Too Much* (New York: Pocket Books, 1985), pp. 279–281.

Handout—Session 1

Five Signs of Addiction*

1. You stay in a bad relationship even when it's hazardous to your health (mental and physical).

2. You give yourself reasons for staying: "I know he really loves me—he just has a different way of showing it."

3. You dread ending the relationship because you believe you'll be alone for life.

4. You suffer withdrawal symptoms when you take steps to end the relationship.

5. When the relationship is over, you feel devastated, lonely, lost—often followed by feelings of exhilaration and freedom.

*Adapted from Howard Halpern, *How to Break Your Addiction to a Person* (New York: McGraw-Hill, 1982), p. 10.

Handout—Session 1

Characteristics of a Woman Who Loves Too Much*

Check (✓) items that you identify with; star (*) items that you are working on.

- ☐ Typically, you come from a dysfunctional home in which your emotional needs were not met.
- ☐ Having received little real nurturing yourself, you try to fill this unmet need vicariously by becoming a caregiver, especially to men who appear needy in some way.
- ☐ Because you were never able to change your parent(s) into the warm, loving caretaker(s) you longed for, you respond deeply to the familiar type of emotionally unavailable man whom you can again try to change through your love.
- ☐ Terrified of abandonment, you'll do anything to keep a relationship from dissolving.
- ☐ Almost nothing is too much trouble, takes too much time, or is too expensive if it will "help" the man with whom you're involved.
- ☐ Accustomed to lack of love in personal relationships, you're willing to wait, hope, and try harder to please.
- ☐ You're willing to take far more than 50% of the responsibility, guilt, and blame in any relationship.
- ☐ Your self-esteem is critically low, and deep inside you don't believe you deserve to be happy. Rather you believe you must earn the right to enjoy life.
- ☐ Having experienced little security in childhood, you have a desperate need to control your men and your relationships. You mask your efforts to control people and situations as "being helpful."
- ☐ In a relationship, you're much more in touch with your dream of how it could be than with the reality of your situation.

- ☐ You may be predisposed emotionally and often biochemically to becoming addicted to drugs, alcohol, and/or certain foods, particularly sugary ones.
- ☐ By being drawn to people with problems that need fixing or by being enmeshed in situations that are chaotic, uncertain, and emotionally painful, you avoid focusing on your responsibility to yourself.
- ☐ You may have a tendency toward experiencing episodes of depression, which you try to forestall through the excitement provided by an unstable relationship.
- ☐ You're not attracted to men who are kind, stable, reliable, and interested in you. You find such "nice" men boring.

*Adapted from Robin Norwood, *Women Who Love Too Much* (New York: Pocket Books, 1985), p. 7.

Handout—Session 1

Characteristics of a Woman Recovered from Loving Too Much*

Check (✓) items that you identify with; star (*) items that you are working on or agree that you will work on.

- ☐ She accepts herself fully, even while wanting to change parts of herself. She has a basic self-love and self-regard, which she carefully nurtures and purposely expands.
- ☐ She accepts others as they are without trying to change them to meet her needs.
- ☐ She's in touch with her feelings and attitudes about every aspect of her life, including her sexuality.
- ☐ She cherishes every aspect of herself—her personality, her appearance, her beliefs and values, her body, her interests and accomplishments. She validates herself rather than searching for a relationship to give her a sense of self-worth.
- ☐ Her self-esteem is great enough that she can enjoy being with others, especially men, who are fine just as they are. She doesn't need to be needed in order to feel worthy.
- ☐ She allows herself to be open and trusting with appropriate people. She's not afraid to be known at a deeply personal level, but she also doesn't expose herself to the exploitation of those who aren't interested in her well-being.
- ☐ She questions, "Is this relationship good for me? Does it enable me to grow into all I am capable of being?"
- ☐ When a relationship is destructive, she's able to let go of it without experiencing disabling depression. She has a circle of supportive friends and healthy interests to see her through crises.
- ☐ She values her own serenity above all else. All the struggles, drama, and chaos of the past have lost their appeal. She's protective of herself, her health, and well-being.

- ☐ She knows that a relationship, in order to work, must be between partners who share similar values, interests, and goals and who each has a capacity for intimacy. She also knows that she's worthy of the best that life has to offer.

*Adapted from Robin Norwood, *Women Who Love Too Much* (New York: Pocket Books, 1985), p. 272.

Handout—Session 1

How Does Your Relationship Rate?*

With your current relationship in mind, read carefully the characteristics of addictive love, then those of mature love. Score your relationship for each characteristic based on the following: 0 = never; 1 = rarely; 2 = sometimes; 3 = often; 4 = almost always; 5 = always. Does your relationship exhibit more symptoms of addictive love than of mature love?

Addictive Love	Mature Love
___ Feels all-consuming	___ Allows for individuality
___ Cannot define ego boundaries	___ Experiences both oneness with and separateness from a lover
___ Is sadomasochistic	___ Brings out best qualities in both partners
___ Fears letting go	___ Accepts endings
___ Fears risk, change, and the unknown	___ Experiences openness to change and exploration
___ Allows little individual growth	___ Invites growth in the other
___ Lacks true intimacy	___ Experiences true intimacy
___ Plays psychological games	___ Feels free to ask honestly for what is wanted
___ Gives in order to get	___ Experiences giving and receiving in the same way
___ Attempts to change the partner	___ Does not attempt to change or control the other
___ Needs the partner to feel complete	___ Encourages self-sufficiency in partner
___ Seeks solutions outside the self	___ Accepts limitations of self and partner
___ Demands and expects unconditional love	___ Does not crave unconditional love
___ Refuses commitment	___ Finds commitment acceptable
___ Looks to the partner for affirmation and worth	___ Has high self-esteem
___ Fears abandonment upon routine separation	___ Trusts memory of beloved; enjoys solitude
___ Recreates old negative feelings	___ Expresses feelings spontaneously
___ Desires, yet fears, closeness	___ Welcomes closeness; risks vulnerability
___ Attempts to take care of the partner's feelings	___ Cares with detachment
___ Plays power games ("one-upmanship")	___ Affirms equality of self and partner

*Adapted with permission from Brenda Schaeffer, *Is It Love or Is It Addiction* (Minneapolis: Hazelden, 1987), pp. 124–125.

Handout—Session 1

Suggested Readings

Beattie, Melody. *Co-Dependent No More.* Minneapolis: Hazelden, 1987.

Black, Claudia. *It Will Never Happen To Me.* Denver: ACT, 1981.

Forward, Susan, & Joan Torres. *Men Who Hate Women and the Women Who Love Them.* New York: Bantam, 1986.

Halpern, Howard. *How To Break Your Addiction to a Person.* New York: McGraw-Hill, 1982.

Lerner, Harriet Goldhor. *The Dance of Anger: A Woman's Guide to Changing the Patterns of Intimate Relationships.* New York: Harper & Row, 1985.

McKay, Matthew, & Patrick Fanning. *Self-Esteem.* Oakland, CA: New Harbinger Publications, 1987.

Norwood, Robin. *Women Who Love Too Much: When You Keep Wishing and Hoping He'll Change.* New York: Pocket Books, 1985.

Norwood, Robin. *Letters to Robin Norwood from Women Who Love Too Much.* New York: Simon & Schuster, 1988.

Peele, Stanton, & Archie Brodsky. *Love and Addiction.* New York: Tapinger, 1975.

Scarf, Maggie. *Intimate Partners: Patterns in Love and Marriage.* New York: Random House, 1987.

Schaeffer, Brenda. *Is It Love or Is It Addiction?* Minneapolis: Hazelden, 1987.

Shakti, Gawain. *Creative Visualization.* New York: Bantam, 1979.

Triere, Lynette, with Richard Peacock. *Learning to Leave: A Woman's Guide.* New York: Warner Books, 1982.

Sanford, Linda Tschirhart, & Mary Donovan. *Women and Self-Esteem.* New York: Penguin Books, 1987.

Wegscheider-Cruse, Sharon. *Choice Making.* Pompano Beach, FL: Health Communications, 1985.

Woititz, Janet. *Struggle for Intimacy.* Pompano Beach, FL: Health Communications, 1985.

SESSION 2
What We Do

OBJECTIVES:

To gain understanding of characteristics of women who love too much (WWLTM) and how they differ from characteristics of women who have recovered.

To identify WWLTM characteristics in myself as well as characteristics of women recovering from loving too much.

To identify priorities for growth and change.

I. OPENING THE SESSION

A. Review of Session 1: Ask members if they wish to comment on previous week's session.

B. Brief overview of Session 2.

II. REVIEW AND DISCUSSION OF HOME ACTIVITIES

A. Review three assessment inventories—Characteristics of a Woman Who Loves Too Much, Characteristics of a Woman Recovered from Loving Too Much, and How Does Your Relationship Rate? (Bring extra copies to session for participants who have forgotten to bring them.)

B. Ask participants if they have any questions regarding the handouts.

C. If many of the members did not do assessment inventories at home, ask them to complete inventories now. Read each item aloud, instructing participants to mark in the appropriate manner. If some participants are still reluctant, ask them to complete the inventories at home for their own information.

D. Review each handout. Participants can refer to these

inventories to help them identify priorities for growth and change in the following exercise.

1. *Characteristics of a Woman Who Loves Too Much*: How many participants identified fewer than five characteristics in themselves? Five to ten? Ten to fifteen? Encourage comments from participants.
2. *Characteristics of a Woman Recovered from Loving Too Much*: Ask each participant to share one characteristic she possesses, takes pride in, or is working on.
3. *How Does Your Relationship Rate*? (Discuss each scale—Addictive Love and Mature Love—separately.)
   - Addictive Love (high scores—60–100—indicate a more addictive relationship): Ask how many participants had scores greater than 50 and how many had less than 50.
   - Mature Love Scale (higher scores indicate less addictive relationship): Ask how many participants had scores greater than 50 and how many had less than 50.

III. EXERCISE ONE: GOAL SETTING AND PRIORITIES FOR GROWTH AND CHANGE

A. Distribute "Seven Steps Out of Love Addiction" handout.

1. Go-round. Read each step aloud. Instruct each participant to read a statement about each step aloud. Instruct participants to think about priority areas they want to work on. After all seven steps are read, ask group to rank the three priority areas numerically, wherein 1 is most important, 2 less important, and 3 least urgent.
2. With a partner or in triads, ask members to share their three priorities with one another. Members should indicate their number-one priority, which they will commit themselves to begin working on immediately. Instruct members to tell their partner(s) why the three priority areas are the most important. Ask them to state what they will do to begin working on the top priority. Encourage participants to be specific. For example, say, "Tomorrow I will . . ." Encourage members to think small, to break larger problems into smaller tasks

that can be worked on, in order to make it possible for them to experience success in small, incremental steps.

3. Encourage members to thank their partner(s) and to express appreciation for their honesty and openness. Encourage members to give one another positive messages about their ability to achieve their goal(s).
4. Reassemble group. In a go-round, ask members to share their number-one priority with the group and what they will do to begin working on this priority. List priorities on flip chart with names: for example,
   Karen—Reprogramming: Be more selfish and do one thing each day to please myself.
   Kate—Exploration: Attend Al-Anon meetings to understand my history.
   Peggy—Reprogramming: I will call someone in the group instead of calling my ex-husband.
5. At the conclusion of the exercise, tell participants that they will be asked to report their progress on their priorities during each of the subsequent sessions.

IV. EXERCISE TWO: VISUALIZING TAKING THAT STEP

A. Ask participants to close their eyes and relax.

B. Say the following: Visualize yourself, in your mind's eye, taking the step that will allow you to free yourself from your love addiction. Make the scene as clear as possible. Where are you? Put in all the sights, sounds, smells. Are you alone? Are you with other people? Fill in the details.

What are you doing? Are you speaking? If you are, what do you hear yourself saying?

Now see yourself taking that step—successfully. Doing what you want to do—reaching your goal. As you reach your goal, notice how you feel. What sensations do you notice in your body? What emotions are you experiencing? Hold on to this scene for a few moments.

Now get ready to return your focus to this room and the group. When you're ready, open your eyes.

C. Discussion: Ask participants what this experience was like for them. Ask them to think about how they could use this experience to help them take the step to achieve their goal. Some suggestions: practice, expand the visual scene, fill in more details.

V. EXERCISE THREE: SENTENCE COMPLETION[1]

A. Objective: To become more aware of who you are as an independent person with your own feelings, thoughts, and wishes.

B. Leader should say the following: I will now ask each of you to spontaneously complete some unfinished statements. Jot down as many responses as you wish to complete each statement. We will then share one of your responses to each statement. For example,

I was . . .	a worthwhile person capable a mess bad, needy, alone
I am . . .	strong independent growing
I will be . . .	stronger more independent

C. Note: Participants whose responses become stuck in negative descriptions are having trouble extricating themselves from addictive thinking.

VI. EXERCISE FOUR: BEING YOUR OWN BEST FRIEND

A. This exercise can be done in triads or in a group.

B. Say the following:

1. Close your eyes. Imagine someone you love or like very much sitting across from you. Imagine telling that person a few things you like about him or her. Silently say

at least three things. Stop when you feel ready to stop. Could you see the person clearly? Was it difficult for you to say these things? How many things did you have to say?

2. Now visualize that you are sitting across from your self facing yourself. Take approximately one minute to tell yourself at least three things you like about yourself. When you're ready, open your eyes.

C. Generate a discussion by asking members the following:
   1. Could you see yourself clearly?
   2. How many of you had difficulty doing this?
   3. How many of you told yourself three or more things?

D. Say the following: Many people have difficulty complimenting themselves, so don't criticize yourself if this exercise was hard for you. Compliments are important for WWLTM because of their tendency to focus on another's well-being and achievements and overlook or discount their own. This pattern interferes with developing a strong sense of one-self—one's own identity and strengths.

   This week, be a good friend to yourself by giving yourself compliments. Become aware of what you like about yourself. You might ask a friend to tell you what he or she likes about you.

   Keep track of compliments you give to yourself and that you receive from others. Write them down in your journal—you might start a special section devoted to compliments. Or drop them in an envelope so that they'll be there for you to read when you need them.

VII. HOME ACTIVITY

A. Distribute "Chart of the Progression of 'Loving Too Much' and Recovery" and "Chart of Alcohol Addiction and Recovery."
   1. Explain how charts are to be read.
   2. Instruct participants to study the "Progression of 'Loving Too Much' and Recovery" chart and to note

where they put themselves on the curve.

3. Instruct participants to compare the similarities between the "Progression of 'Loving Too Much' and Recovery" chart and the "Alcohol Addiction and Recovery" chart.

B. Remind members to work on their number one priority as well as on taking that step they agreed to take.

C. Tell members to keep track of the compliments they receive. Encourage participants to give themselves some compliments.

VIII. CLOSING

Read the following meditation or ask group members to read: "I want to get you excited about who you are, what you are, what you have, and what can still be for you. I want to inspire you to see that you can go far beyond where you are right now."

"We can actively create excitement and inspiration in our lives. We need not wait for them to come to us. That's one of the choices we have as human beings, as women."

"Passively waiting for "the good life" represents old, worn out, past behavior. Each day we can set our sights on reaching a goal. We can take a step or two toward that goal. Progress is there for the making, achievement is there for the taking. Whatever our hearts' pure desires, we can move toward that goal. We are what we need to be. We have what we need to move ahead."

"Today, I will let my excitement for life's possibilities spur me on."[2]

References

1. Howard Halpern, *How to Break Your Addiction to a Person* (New York: McGraw-Hill, 1982).
2. *Meditations for Women* (Minneapolis: Hazelden, 1982).

HANDOUT—SESSION 2

Seven Steps Out of Love Addiction*

1. **AWARENESS:**
   Admit that love addiction plays a role in your life.
   Make overcoming love addiction the most important priority in your life.

2. **ASSESSMENT:**
   Discover the degree of your addiction.
   Go for help.
   Find a support group of peers who understand.

3. **DECISION:**
   Use your personal power to move from dependence to true love.
   Telephone therapy with people you relate to in the group.

4. **EXPLORATION:**
   Examine your personal fears, myths, and history.
   Courageously face your own problems and shortcomings.

5. **REPROGRAMMING:**
   Let go of the old; embrace the new.
   Stop managing and controlling others.
   Learn not to get "hooked" into relationship games.
   Become more selfish; be yourself without trying to please others.

6. **EXPANSION:**
   Develop your personal uniqueness and the ability to truly love yourself and others.

7. **RENEWAL:**
   Move toward development of mature love relationships.

*Adapted with permission from Brenda Schaeffer, *Is It Love or Is It Addiction* (Minneapolis: Hazelden, 1987); Robin Norwood, *Women Who Love Too Much* (New York: Pocket Books, 1985).

Handout—Session 2
To be read from left to right

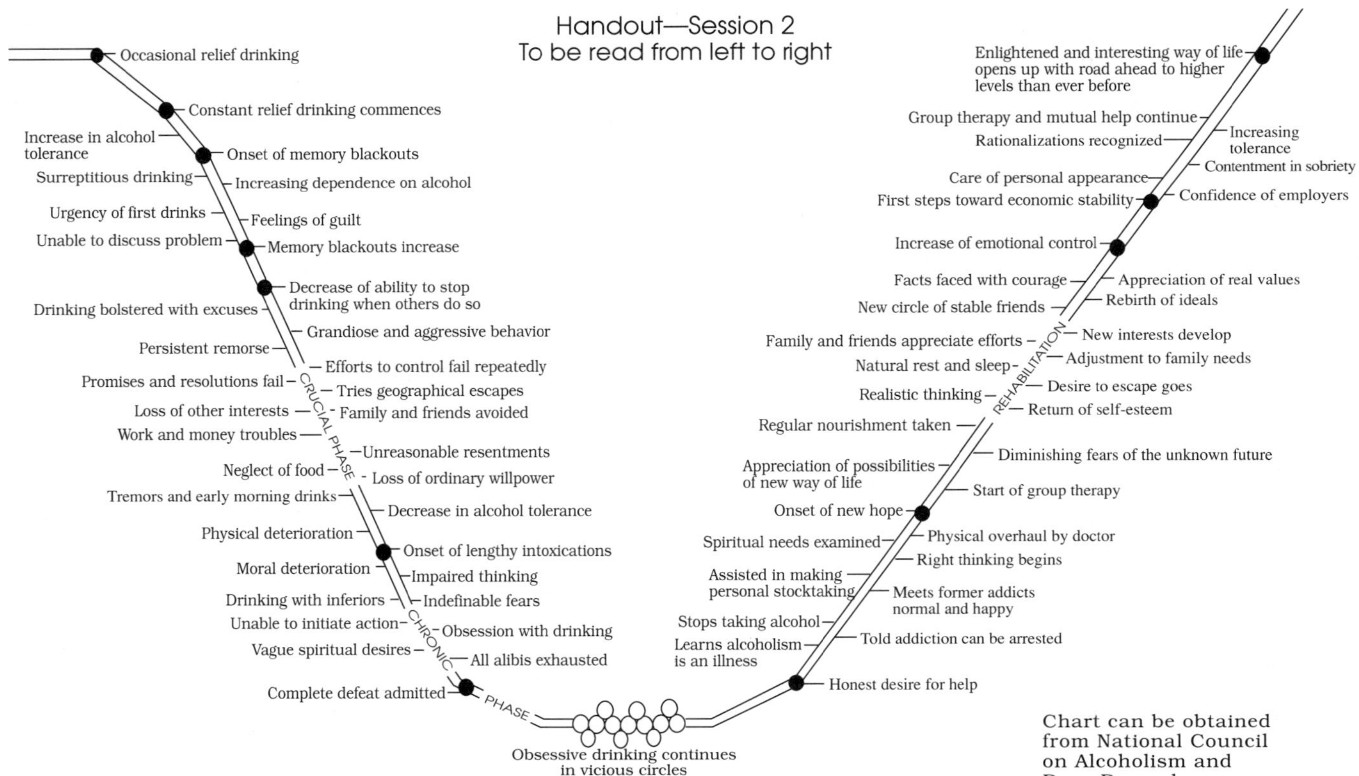

Chart can be obtained from National Council on Alcoholism and Drug Dependence

A Chart of Alcohol Addiction and Recovery
Adapted from M. M. Glatt, *British Journal of Addiction* 54 (2)

Handout—Session 2
To be read from left to right

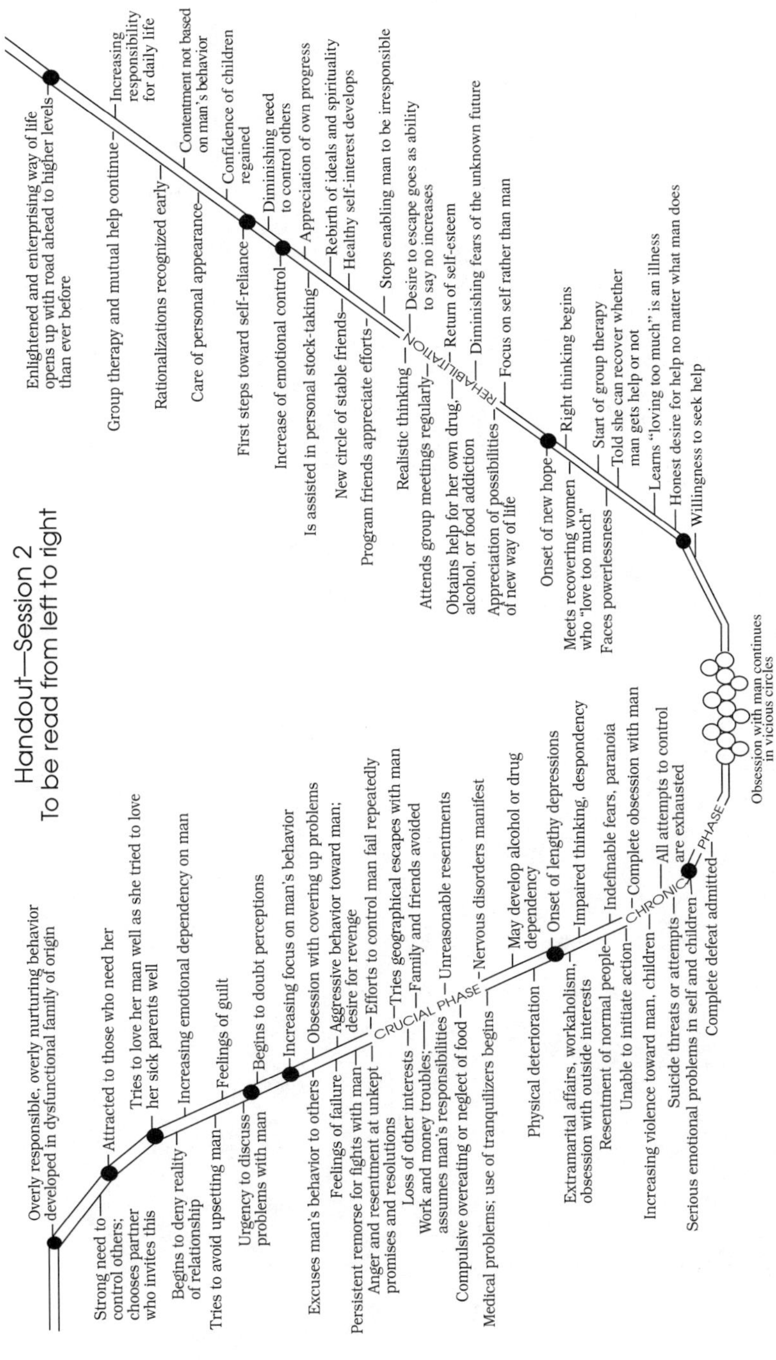

A Chart of the Progression of "Loving Too Much" and Recovery

Adapted from Robin Norwood, *Women Who Love Too Much* (New York: Pocket Books, 1985), p. 213.

SESSION 3
Why We Do It

OBJECTIVES:

To understand how our efforts to overcome negative past experiences leave us vulnerable to choosing relationships that are unhealthy and that become addictive.

To learn about and to practice giving ourselves positive affirmations that will raise self-esteem and help us to achieve our goals.

I. OPENING THE SESSION

A. Review of Session 2: Ask members if they wish to comment on previous week's session.

B. Brief overview of Session 3.

II. REVIEW AND DISCUSSION OF HOME ACTIVITIES

A. Review "Progression of 'Loving Too Much' and Recovery" chart.
   1. Ask members if they were able to place themselves along the curve.
   2. Encourage discussion.

B. Review "Alcohol Addiction and Recovery" chart.
   1. Ask members if they were able to perceive the similarities between alcohol addiction and love addiction.
   2. Encourage discussion.

C. Ask members if they were able to take positive steps toward achieving the goal(s) that they established during previous week's session. Encourage discussion.

D. Ask members if they kept track of compliments they received during the week. Ask them if they took time to compliment themselves.

E. Again encourage members to use one another for support by calling one another or meeting during the week.

III. AFFIRMING YOURSELF

A. Mini-Lecture[1]
Most people need support and encouragement to make changes. One of the most effective ways to create a supportive environment for growth and change is to give affirmations to yourself. Affirmations are positive, loving statements you tell yourself. You can say them aloud, silently, or write them down. Affirmations counteract negative thoughts—your own self-criticisms or negative messages collected from others. They can help you be kinder to yourself and more self-appreciative. Affirmations acknowledge your strong qualities and help you achieve a success-focused outlook. Affirmations may be thought of as a gift you can give yourself at any time. If you depend only on someone else's approval before you allow yourself to feel good about yourself, your self-esteem will swing wildly between highs and lows. Instead, accept and approve of yourself. When you do receive approval from others, so much the better. But you don't have to rely on another person to make you feel good. You can do it for yourself.

Self-affirmations help you create a more positive and loving self-image and also help you achieve what you want out of life. They help transform negative attitudes and expectations and allow you to create a more satisfying life. Affirmations are useful for increasing confidence, raising self-esteem, improving relationships, helping you in your job or career, overcoming self-defeating thoughts, and empowering you to achieve your goals.

B. Exercise One: Self-Affirmations
1. Leader should state the following:
For this exercise, think about specific qualities that you appreciate in yourself. Or think of a quality you want for yourself or goals you desire, then create

your own affirmations to help you realize these ends. Instruct participants to use the following format to affirm themselves:
"I, (group leader's name), love and appreciate myself just as I am."
Group should respond:
"You, (group leader's name), love and appreciate yourself just as you are."

Suggest other examples to the group:
I, ____, am talented, intelligent, and creative.
I, ____, am sensitive, warm, and friendly.
I, ____, welcome new experiences.

Going around the room, ask each member to make a self-affirmation. Tell members to think of goals they desire and design affirmations that will create themselves as they want to be. For example,
I, ____, now have enough time, energy, wisdom, and money to accomplish my desires.
I, ____, now have a satisfying, well-paying job.
I, ____, express myself clearly and effectively to everyone.

Instruct group to respond as described above.

2. Distribute "Wellness Affirmation" handout. Review instructions and ask members to complete it in class.

3. After members have completed the handout, the leader should state the following: Affirmations are stated positively and in the present, as if the change has been made. Don't say: "I will stop eating junk food." Say, "I am now enjoying a healthy diet every day." Writing affirmations down can be a very effective technique. Write affirmations over and over, filling a page or more. For added power, use your name and write the affirmation in the first, second, and third person. For example,
I, ____, am growing more physically fit every day.
You, ____, are growing more physically fit every day.
She, ____, is growing more physically fit every day.

If doubts come up as you write, turn the page over and write the doubts down. For example, you might think, "I've never stayed long enough with an exercise program to benefit before, so I probably won't succeed now." Write an answer to this doubt that is realistic and encouraging: "That was the past. Today is a new day. I can change." Then turn the page back and fine tune your affirmation to fit comfortably with the doubts or negative feelings. Imagine your life as if the affirmation were already a reality. Repeat this exercise several times a day until the new belief feels natural to you or you achieve your goal. We become what we believe about ourselves. Remember, you possess the power to change your life!

IV. MASTERING THE PAST—THE MYTH[2]

A. Mini-Lecture: Dysfunctional Learning

People whose childhood was filled with unhappy and painful experiences often feel compelled to recreate the same painful experiences in their adult life. We do this because we believe in the myth that we can gain mastery over these painful experiences if only we work hard enough. The myth is played out as follows:

- Replay the old memories, only use a new cast of characters.
- Our goal—to win the old battle, to be loved today as we never were loved as children.
- If our efforts don't work with one partner, find another partner and try again, even harder, as many times as it takes. Perhaps we'll do better, we think, if we just try harder and love more.

We are compelled to fight and to win this old battle from the past. Its hold over us is very powerful, especially if our past was extremely painful. The myth keeps us searching for someone who's the mirror image of our parents—one who doesn't easily show us love but who, we believe, we can make love us if we only love him more. Over and over again we are compulsively attracted to the same situations and relationships. And repeatedly we keep trying harder to be loved by a person who may be emotionally unavailable, abusive, or addicted to alcohol or drugs. It doesn't work! Instead of finding the love we crave, we only get hurt.

Why don't we know how to choose appropriate partners? It's because when we were growing up we did not learn the skills that would help us choose partners who are good for us—partners who would allow us to grow and with whom we could have a healthy love relationship. We didn't learn the skills that would help us develop mature relationships. In fact, we learned how to develop dysfunctional relationships.

We already know that in dysfunctional families—and perhaps in our own families—our emotional needs for love and affection were not met. We received little time or attention. We learned how to relate to others in ways that undermine healthy relationships and our own developmental needs. More specifically, we learned the following rules:

1. *Don't talk about important problems*: Under this rule, the reality of your problems (inside or outside the family) was denied, as if your problems didn't exist. The degree of denial and secrecy surrounding problems determined how dysfunctional the family was and how unprepared for healthy relationships the members became.
2. *Don't step outside your place or role:* In dysfunctional families, roles are rigid. The message is "Know your place and stay there! I'm the parent, you're the child (regardless of age)! You're not free to express differences, needs, feelings. I'm the man, you're the woman; do what I say!" In dysfunctional families, what you do or say is determined by your role in the family.
3. *Don't question the rules*: In dysfunctional families, members must obey rigid, inflexible rules. The rules of the adults can never be questioned.

B. Discussion

The leader should encourage discussion by asking the group the following questions: Can you recall any messages you were given as a child that highlight the three rules of the dysfunctional family? For example, were there things that you knew or were told you couldn't talk about? Were you told to stay in your place?

Ask the group to provide examples, such as

- Mother/father knows best!
- No back talk!
- Do as I say, I'm the mother/father!
- Stop asking so many questions.
- Who do you think you are?
- Whatever made you think that? Where did you get that crazy idea?
- You're getting too big for your britches.
- Obey/respect your parents.
- Mind your own business.

The consequences of these messages can be disastrous for relationships. What are the consequences? (List responses on a blackboard or chart paper.)
Examples include

- Rejection, criticism, and/or violence.
- You learn to distrust your own thoughts and feelings; your reality is denied. As a result, you stop thinking, and your self-esteem is diminished.
- You lack the tools and skills to evaluate new situations and relationships. You fail to learn the skills of discussion, questioning, considering pros/cons, problem solving.

As a child, you have no way of knowing what's good or bad for you, so you learn to play it safe. This tendency carries over into adult life. You avoid new experiences and stick close to what you know, even though doing so isn't good for you. You're attracted to what's familiar, and "what's familiar" is harmful for you. You don't know how to appraise and handle unfamiliar situations and relationships. You learn to obey the rules, stay in your place, and not talk about important problems. You feel discouraged and feel unable to develop yourself or expand your experiences and relationships outside that which you learned growing up. Thus, it's not surprising that you become very frightened of the unknown. And the big unknown for WWLTM is establishing healthy relationships with partners who will not exploit or mistreat them.

Questions for discussion:

1. What messages did you hear as a child that stressed the three rules (don'ts) of the dysfunctional family?
2. How are these rules (don'ts) being played out in your adult life?

C. Mini-Lecture: It Feels So Right!

- Why is it that women who need to be needed find men who are looking for someone to take care of them?
- Why is it that women who are self sacrificing find men who are very selfish?
- Why is it that women who see themselves as being weak, helpless—as victims—find men who see themselves as powerful and aggressive?
- Why is it that women who need to control someone find men who are inadequate?

Two factors set the stage for these kinds of relationships:

1. The woman's relationship patterns that she learned as a child fit the partner's familiar patterns—like putting together pieces of a jigsaw puzzle.
2. The woman's compulsion to recreate relationships so she can overcome the painful experiences of her childhood.

If we're addicted to a particular type of relationship—perhaps with men who are needy, emotionally distant, demanding, abusive, or alcoholic—when we meet a new man, our antennae are tuned to pick up signals that tell us that this man is familiar, this man feels "right." We feel we belong together. A WWLTM experiences a flash of instant recognition when she meets a man who allows her to experience the old familiar feelings that she felt when she was growing up. Even though the relationship may be dysfunctional, she feels comfortable and "at home" with this man because she knows all the moves to make, despite the fact that they result in pain and didn't work before. For example, if he has a short fuse and a terrible temper, she'll humor him, keep it light, keep him amused, and never do or say anything that will trigger an explosion. The WWLTM is unaware that she has become obsessed with trying to change a man who, perhaps, is just like her angry, abusive father. She tells herself, "This time, I'll make it work!" That's the attraction, the challenge, and the delusion.

D. Questions for Discussion

1. What felt familiar and right for you when you were first attracted to your partner?
2. Were you and your partner concerned about or did you have fights about issues similar to those that caused problems in your childhood home? For example, sex, money, fidelity, children, relatives, outside interests, power and control, independence, responsibility?

E. Mini-Lecture: The Chemistry That Keeps Us Hooked

So we found the man who feels right and familiar. What's the chemistry, the electricity, the spark that keeps us hooked in a relationship that's so unsatisfying, even harmful for us?

The hook is the constant challenge and struggle to change a man who is not O.K. just as he is.[3] We believe in the myth that our love has the power to change him into the man we want. This belief fuels and validates our struggle. He becomes the focus of our life, an all-consuming project into which we pour our energy, attention, resources, and creativity. Our dissatisfaction with the way he is and our efforts to change him often create conflict in the relationship. Tension builds. The relationship is filled with insecurity and unpredictability. All this effort, drama, and excitement may keep us so stimulated and busy dancing to his tune that we are distracted from our own unhappiness. We fail to recognize our own low self-esteem. In focusing our life on reacting to the problems caused by his dysfunctional behavior, we create excitement in our life; the adrenalin flows and we become hooked—both physically and emotionally.

Is this the kind of excitement you want in your life?

V. EXERCISE TWO: AWARENESS EXERCISE—MR. NICE GUY

Ask group members to respond to the following question with a show of hands:

"Have you ever said to yourself, 'He's such a nice guy, but oh, what a bore' or 'He just doesn't excite me—he's too nice'?"[4]

How many of you ever had a Mr. Nice Guy in your life at one time or another? Or more than one? Or wished for one? A nice guy is O.K. just as he is. There's nothing about him you need to change.

Close your eyes and recall Mr. Nice Guy or create your own imaginary Mr. Nice Guy. Pay attention to his appearance—what does he look like? Now put yourself in the picture. Focus on the interaction between the two of you. What's happening? What's the experience like for you? What do you feel? What do you like about him, what do you dislike?

Now on a scale from 0 to 10, in which 0 means you feel no attraction and 10 means you feel very attracted, rate your attraction to him.

Now, open your eyes. Take a piece of paper. At the top of the page write "Mr. Nice Guy." Divide the paper vertically in half. You could simply fold it and reopen it. At the top of the left column, write, "I LIKE," and on the right side, "I DISLIKE." Now under these headings, list the qualities you like and dislike about Mr. Nice Guy.

A. In triads ask members to share and discuss what they wrote. Discuss the following questions:
1. Was this a man whom I'd like to know better?
2. What beliefs about yourself (or message from the past) would you need to change for you to feel interested in, attracted to, and able to welcome and enjoy a Mr. Nice Guy in your life?
3. Could you create an affirmation that supports this change?

B. In group, taking a positive focus, the leader should list what members liked about Mr. Nice Guy. Discuss with the group how they might increase their interest in Mr. Nice Guy. Discuss what beliefs about themselves would need to be changed before they could establish a relationship with Mr. Nice Guy.

VI. HOME ACTIVITIES

Instruct members to continue their work on goals and priorities.

VII. CLOSING

Group member or group leader reads meditation. Or use other method of closing that you prefer. Be creative.

REFERENCES

1. Shakti Gawain, *Creative Visualization* (New York: Bantam-New Age, 1979).
2. Robin Norwood, *Women Who Love Too Much* (New York: Pocket Books, 1985).
3. Ibid.
4. Ibid.

Handout—Session 3

Wellness Affirmation*

To enter into and sustain a healthy love relationship, one must be complete in oneself and living a life of wellness. Wellness in our context means knowing how to meet one's needs and not looking outside the self to find completeness.

Read slowly the following affirmations, personalizing them by inserting your name. If an affirmation feels out of sync, then you may need to explore the disharmony, for it hints at a vulnerable spot in your relationship(s).

I,____, now know what my real needs are and how to meet them.
I,____, am now freely and effectively expressing my feelings to others.
I,____, am acting assertively and in ways that consider the feelings and freedom of others.
I,____, am enjoying my body by means of good nutrition, adequate exercise, and physical awareness.
I,____, am engaged in activities that are meaningful to me and reflect my inner values.
I,____, am creating and enjoying close, intimate relationships with others.
I,____, am responding to challenges in life as opportunities for growth in strength and maturity.
I,____, am creating the life I want, rather than reacting to whatever happens.
I,____, am using physical signals to see improvement and increase my self-knowledge.
I,____, am enjoying a sense of well-being even in times of adversity.
I,____, know my own inner emotional and physical patterns and understand them to be signals from my inner self.
I,____, trust my own personal resources as the greatest strength for living and growing.
I,____, am experiencing myself as a wonderful person.
I,____, am creating situations that help me realize my personal worth.
I,____, believe there is abundance in life for me.

*Adapted with permission from Brenda Schaeffer, *Is It Love Or Is It Addiction?* (Minneapolis: Hazelden, 1987), pp. 147-148.

SESSION 4
Letting Go of Old Relationship Patterns

OBJECTIVES:

To identify old dysfunctional patterns in your relationships and to consider how you might change your style of loving to a more satisfying way of relating.
To increase your ability to take better care of yourself in your relationships and in your life.

I. OPENING THE SESSION

A. Review of Session 3: Ask members if they wish to comment on previous week's session.

B. Brief overview of Session 4.

II. MINI-LECTURE: LETTING GO OF OLD ROLES

Women who love too much need to let go of old roles, old patterns of relating with others, that they learned while growing up. Often, WWLTM tend to assume one or a combination of several of the following roles.

- Overly responsible, needing to be in charge.
- Overly nurturing of others, failing to consider their own needs.
- Overly focused on the behavior of other people, ignoring their own growth and developmental needs.

Women who love too much need to develop new patterns of relating with others. If they are to establish healthy, mutually satisfying relationships, they must learn to

- focus their attention on their own needs, not just the needs of their partner.
- develop healthy outside interests that are gratifying to themselves.

- give to and care for themselves, not just take care of the needs of others.[1]

In the next few minutes, as I describe each role, think about whether you play this role, and if you do, how well the role really works for you in your life. Consider whether it might make good sense for you to learn new coping skills that allow you to relate to others in healthier, more satisfying ways. Now, let's look at these roles we continuously try to make work for us.

III. MINI-LECTURE: THE OVERRESPONSIBLE ROLE

How many of you need to be in control, to take charge of situations and relationships? (Ask for a show of hands.) What are some of the reasons people assume this role?

Being in control makes people feel secure, makes their life seem more predictable. Perhaps as a child, you had to take charge, assume more responsibility than you should have had to, just to help the family survive. Perhaps you experienced sudden and dramatic upheavals in your home life and you had to take charge in order to establish some semblance of order in your family life. Because your security was threatened as a child, when things get out of control now, you feel insecure. Life must feel predictable before you feel secure. If you don't know what to expect, it's difficult for you to make plans. If you feel that situations are getting out of control, you become afraid of losing control of your feelings.[2]

Of course, feeling a sense of self-control and mastery over life situations is necessary and desirable. However, if the only way you can feel good about yourself is when you are in control and running the show, then you run the risk of being overburdened and overworked. You may experience a high level of stress and run the risk of developing stress-related illnesses. What's more, you may end up harming the very relationships you are trying to protect. Ultimately, life is not predictable. Women who assume this role need to learn to let go of themselves and others, to learn to roll with life's punches. But how do you let go when you've spent your whole life trying to maintain control?

First, by realizing that there's no reason to always have to be responsible, the person in control, when the family appears to be functioning well.

Second, you must learn to recognize, experience, and accept your own feelings. *Own* your feelings, accept the fact that at various times you're going to feel sad, angry, frustrated, happy—then learn to express these feelings in ways that feel positive and safe.

Third, take time to learn about yourself. Let others assume some of life's responsibilities and give yourself the opportunity to develop your own interests and activities.

Exercise One

1. Distribute "The Overresponsible Role" handout.
2. Moving around the group, ask each member to read the new messages aloud.
3. Ask members to share the messages that seem most important for them to work on.

IV. MINI-LECTURE: THE CARETAKER ROLE[3]

Many women learned at a tender age that to be a woman is to help others. Helping others is an admirable human trait and is often necessary for survival. However, it becomes a problem when people fail to take care of themselves as well as others.

Some of us grew up with a compulsive need to nurture. Maybe we had to grow up too fast and assumed too much responsibility too soon. Maybe we were more like parents than children when we were young. Maybe we filled in for a parent who was absent due to death, divorce, physical illness, or emotional instability. Or perhaps our parents were preoccupied with marital conflict or other problems. Maybe we had no choice but to help care for our brothers and sisters and even our parent(s). We learned very early how to take care of everyone. Everyone, that is, but ourselves. Our own needs, our own wants came second—if they were considered at all. Now, as adults, we continue to play this role. We keep searching for the opportunity to do what we know and feel we are good at—helping and nurturing others while hoping to get some measure of love in return. A woman who plays the caretaker role believes that she's loved only for her nurturing qualities, not for who she is in and of herself. Because her self-esteem is low, the only way she can feel good about herself is through the services she performs for others.

A woman with a compulsive need to nurture goes far beyond giving help when it is wanted and needed. Rather, she becomes a caretaker/rescuer. She's attracted to men who are wounded, needy, with problems—men she believes she can take care of and rescue. A person is a rescuer or caretaker when she takes responsibility for another person's thoughts, feelings, decisions, problems, well-being, future —in other words, when she doesn't allow others to take responsibility for themselves.

Distribute "Examples of Caretaker Behaviors" handout.[4]
Read to group.

- Doing something we really don't want to do
- Saying yes when we mean no
- Doing something for someone although that person is capable of and should be doing it for him- or herself
- Meeting people's needs without being asked and before we've agreed to do so
- Speaking for another person
- Solving people's problems for them
- Not asking for what we want, need, and desire
- Doing more than a fair share of work after our help is requested
- Consistently giving more than we receive in a particular situation
- Fixing people's feelings
- Doing people's thinking for them
- Suffering people's consequences for them
- Putting more interest and activity into a joint effort than the other person does

But the caretaker role has a dark side. Have you ever had the experience of struggling with something you were trying to fix, perhaps a broken appliance, or perhaps having some difficulty finding a convenient repair shop in the Yellow Pages, when, in the midst of your effort, a friend comes up to you and says, "Oh, let me do that for you!"

After initially feeling grateful (maybe!) for the help, did you experience any negative feelings? What were they?

Perhaps you suddenly felt incompetent, which, in turn, may have made you feel resentful and angry. Perhaps you snapped (or felt like snapping) at your friend, "I can do it myself. I'm not helpless, you know." And perhaps your friend became angry in return, saying, "I'm only trying to help." Or, if your friend was a bit more sensitive, "I'm sorry, that was stupid of me. I know you can do it."

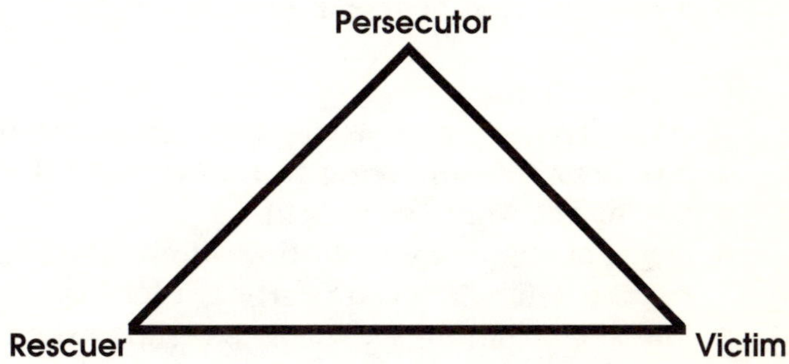

Stephen Karpman, a professional who has studied human relationships, devised something he calls the Karpman Triangle.[5] Karpman points out that rescuing someone is not always the friendliest or nicest thing someone can do for another person. Rescuing someone presumes that (1) someone is a victim, (2) the rescuer is competent, and (3) the victim is incompetent.

Given the scenario described above, in which a friend barges in and assumes responsibility for a problem you were trying to solve, where would you place yourself and your friend on the triangle? Where would you place the feelings and reactions listed below?

Negative feelings	Reaction	Friend's reaction
felt incompetent	snapped at friend	angry
resentful	angry	apologized

A. Negative Feelings of Caretakers/Rescuers
Have you ever agreed to do something for someone even though you didn't want to? Why did you agree? What were some of your feelings? Did you feel resentful and angry at the person for asking you to do something you didn't want to? Did you take out your resentment and anger on the person?

How might the other person then react to your reactions? Did he or she counter with "you could have said no!"

How might you react to this counterattack? By apologizing, saying, "I'm sorry, I had no right to snap at you."

B. Discussion
How can we avoid playing this caretaker/rescuer game?

- Before volunteering your help, ask the person if he or she wants your help.
- If others ask you for help, don't hesitate to ask them for help when you need it.
- Don't volunteer your help if you don't want to or don't have the time to help.
- Learn how to say "no."

C. Exercise Two

1. Distribute "The Caretaker Role" handout.
2. Moving around the group, ask each member to read the new messages aloud.
3. Ask members to share the messages that seem most important for them to work on.

D. Exercise Three
In dyads or as a group, instruct members to discuss the following questions:

1. Do you consider yourself a "goody two-shoes"? Are you always a "goody two-shoes"?
2. Have you ever served as a caretaker for an extended period? What is your earliest memory of being a caretaker?
3. What do others say about your caretaking? Are you praised/criticized? How do you feel about their comments?
4. Do you ever think the following: "If I don't take care of this person, he or she won't care about me."
5. Does your self-esteem depend on your caretaking?
6. Think about alternative ways to develop your self-esteem. Ask yourself, "What other attractive qualities do I possess in addition to caretaking?" Think about your skills, talents, your capacity to learn and grow, your sense of humor, energy, spirituality, sexiness. List them. How could you spend more time and energy developing these potential new sources of self-esteem?
7. How does defining your role as that of a caretaker while disowning your other qualities affect your relationships and your life?
8. On a scale of 0–10, how important is caretaking to your self-esteem?

E. Exercise Four
Perform the following exercise as a group.

Close your eyes. Ask yourself the following: What other attractive qualities do I possess in addition to caretaking? Consider your skills, talents, capacity to learn and grow, sense of humor, spirituality, energy, sexiness.

Open your eyes. Jot these qualities down on a piece of paper. Choose one quality to share with the group.

Ask each member to share this quality with the group.

F. Exercise Five
Break into dyads. Instruct participants to discuss their list of attractive qualities with each other. Each

partner should take approximately two minutes to describe her qualities. Instruct partners to discuss for approximately five minutes how they might spend more time and energy developing these potential new sources of self-esteem. With entire group discuss the ideas they developed for enhancing their sources of self-esteem.

V. THE SUPERADAPTABLE ROLE[6]

People who play the superadaptable role want to remain invisible. They don't want to draw any attention to their own qualities, their own needs. They constantly adapt themselves to others' wants and needs. Their goal is to be as nonassertive and as flexible as possible. In so doing, the superadaptable one loses touch with her own feelings and needs, becomes passive, detached, and nondescript. The super-adaptable person has no direction or goals.

A. Exercise Six[7]
Break into dyads. The goal of this exercise is to develop your ability to make choices in your life as well as to identify your own sense of "power" over your life.

With your partner, make two lists of options: (1) for a typical day and (2) over a longer period. The first list should describe options that are routine, easy. List as many as you can and don't be afraid to be trivial. For example, I have the option to choose

- what time I will get up in the morning
- whether I will take a walk before breakfast
- what I will do on my lunch break
- whether to read or watch television in the evening
- what I will eat for dinner

Make a second list of more challenging options. For example, I have the option to choose

- how much time I will devote to my family and how much time I will allow for myself
- whether to invite a friend to dinner or to see a new play
- whether to enroll in a class or workshop

- whether to paint a room
- whether to seek a new job

Now make a list of options you did not take. For example, I chose not to exercise my power when

- I went to see a film chosen by my friend that I did not wish to see
- I did not return a badly pressed dress to the dry cleaners to be redone
- I did not return a defective item to the store as the defect was minor

Discuss with your partner how you might expand your awareness of the options in your life. Your feeling of personal power will grow as you become aware of the many choices you have available to you, whether or not you choose to act on them.

Reassemble the group and ask participants for suggestions on how they can increase their awareness of options in their life.

B. Exercise Seven

1. Distribute "The Superadaptable Role" handout.
2. Moving around group, ask each member to read the new messages aloud.
3. Ask members to share the message(s) that seem most important for them to work on.

C. Exercise Eight

Instruct members to make a list of situations in which they reacted by adapting to another's wishes. Ask members also to write out what they could have done to become an "actor," that is, an equal participant in the decision and activity. For example,

Reactor	**Actor**
When partner decides where you should go on vacation	Express your ideas of what you should do. Gather information about things to do and places to go to support your ideas.

When partner decides how money should be spent	Give your opinion. Develop budget together. Pay the bills. Balance the checkbook.
When your partner makes holiday plans	Assert your preference. Offer to negotiate differences.
When partner decides what chores he will do and not do	Initiate planning of chores according to fairness, skill, and time availability. Rotate chores that both of you dislike.

D. Exercise Nine

1. As a group, ask members to do the following: think about what it would be like for you if you let someone else make decisions and take charge in areas of your life that you now control—at home, at work, in your relationships. Now ask yourself: what areas of control or what activities might you be willing to give up? Pick one area or activity that would be relatively easy for you to give up, that you might let someone else handle. If you can't get yourself to let go of a responsibility, try letting go of feeling responsible for how other people are feeling.
2. Break into dyads. Tell your partner what responsibility or area of control you might give up and what you think might happen if you gave up this responsibility. Weigh the positives and negatives. What might you gain? What might you lose? Divide paper into two columns and record the plusses on one side and the minuses on the other.
3. Discuss with your partner the area of responsibility you plan to give up control of during the following week. It can be the responsibility you already discussed or a different one.
4. As group discuss the following:
   - What responsibility will members let go of?
   - What might happen?
   - Ask members to report on their progress during the next session.
   - Ask them beliefs they would need to change for them to let go of responsibility more often. For

example, "I, and only I, know the best way to do things" or, "The only way to feel good about myself is to be in charge or to do it myself."

E. Free Time

If you give up control or responsibility over something, you will have more free time. Consider this free time as playtime—something that, perhaps, you had little of as a child. Very responsibile and serious children become very responsible and serious adults. Obviously, being responsible is a necessary part of life. However, one must know how to play and have fun as well. Use your free time to change your pattern of being overresponsible to a pattern that lets you be spontaneous and fun loving. Let the kid in you out to relax, laugh, feel good, and have fun. Play and fun are a necessary and healthy part of life.

Ask yourself what you might do to have fun. What can you do that does not involve being overresponsible or in control? (Leader might add the following.)

- Take a walk
- Ride a bicycle
- Visit a museum or art gallery
- Relax on the beach
- Sit under a tree
- Listen to a relaxation tape
- Watch the moon rise, the sun rise or set
- Give and receive a massage
- Go out for breakfast
- Blow bubbles
- Sketch, paint, play with modeling clay
- Join a chorus
- Join a theater group
- Play music
- Take an arts and craft class

F. Exercise Ten

Distribute "Fun Activities" handout and ask members to do either in class or at home.

VI. VISUALIZATION: LETTING GO OF OLD ROLES

As a group, ask members to do the following: Relax. Close your eyes. Take a deep breath and let it out slowly. Follow your breath down through your body and out your toes.

Visualize a typical situation in which you are playing the role of either the overresponsible one, the caretaker, or the over-adaptable one. Notice whom you are with, where you are, what is happening. Develop the details of your surroundings—are you indoors or outdoors? What colors do you see? What sounds do you hear? What odors do you smell? Notice how your body feels.

While visualizing yourself acting out your old role in the scene you are visualizing, begin changing your actions—what you do and say. You feel more self-aware than before. You are taking care of yourself, loving, nurturing and pleasing yourself. You feel very, very good about that. You begin feeling a new responsibility to yourself; you know that no one but you can know what's really best for you. Feel the contentment that comes with taking responsibility for your own well-being and happiness as you give up the old stale roles that no longer work for you.

Continue to visualize this scene for a few moments. Enjoy it. When you are ready, open your eyes.

Ask group to share their experience of this visualization. Encourage members to practice this visualization technique daily.

VII. RESPONSES OF OTHERS TO YOUR CHANGING ROLE PATTERNS

When you start making more decisions for yourself, become more assertive, and begin saying "no" to requests you consider unreasonable or intrusive, others will respond to you differently. Many will like the change and make adjustments in the relationship. Others may attempt to manipulate or sabotage the "new you" so that you'll continue to take care of them and do what they want. Don't give up; eventually, most people will accept your new way of relating to them. And regardless of how others respond to you, you'll like yourself better when you give more to yourself and develop yourself more fully.

Role	**Goal**
Overresponsible	Be more spontaneous; be willing to be a follower sometimes.
Superadaptable	Be more assertive; say what you think/feel/want.
Caretaker/Rescuer	Allow others to take more responsibility for themselves. Give help only when wanted or needed, and when you really want to give it.

As group, do closing ritual.

References

1. Claudia Black, *It Will Never Happen to Me* (Denver: ACT, 1982).
2. Ibid.
3. Maggie Scarf, *Intimate Partners: Patterns in Love and Marriage* (New York: Random House, 1987); Melodie Beattie, *Co-Dependent No More* (Minneapolis: Hazelden, 1987); Robin Norwood, *Women Who Love Too Much* (New York: Pocket Books, 1985).
4. Beattie, *Co-Dependent No More*, pp. 78–79.
5. Ibid., pp. 77–78; Stephen B. Karpman, "Script Drama Analysis," *Transactional Analysis Bulletin*, 26 (1968): 39–43.
6. Black, *It Will Never Happen to Me*, pp. 127–32.
7. Ibid., pp. 128–29

Handout—Session 4

The Overresponsible Role

New Messages:

- I don't have to be so responsible, serious, and in control all the time.
- Sometimes I can feel good being a follower.
- I have feelings of fear and anger and that's O.K.
- I deserve to have some fun in my life.

Handout—Session 4

Examples of Caretaker Behaviors*

- Doing something we really don't want to do
- Saying yes when we mean no
- Doing something for someone although that person is capable of and should be doing it for him- or herself
- Meeting people's needs without being asked or before we've agreed to do so
- Speaking for another person
- Solving people's problems for them
- Not asking for what we want, need, and desire
- Doing more than a fair share of work after our help is requested
- Consistently giving more than we receive in a particular situation
- Fixing people's feelings
- Doing people's thinking for them
- Suffering people's consequences for them
- Putting more interest and activity into a joint effort than the other person does

*Adapted with permission from Melodie Beattie, *Co-Dependent No More* (Minneapolis: Hazelden, 1987), pp. 78–79.

Handout—Session 4

The Caretaker Role

New Messages:

- I don't HAVE to take care of everyone.
- My needs are important.
- It's O.K. to put my own well-being first.
- I'm NOT GUILTY when others feel bad.

Handout—Session 4

The Superadaptable Role

New Messages:

- I'm a very important person.
- I have a right to assert myself.
- Sometimes it's healthier and more satisfying not to be so flexible.

Handout—Session 4

Fun Activities*

List fun activities you've always wanted to do, even though you seldom have had the opportunity to do them in the past. Ask yourself if it is possible for you to participate in any of these activities. Circle the ones that you could do easily. Then double circle the ones you are willing to try next week. Start doing them!

1. __________
2. __________
3. __________
4. __________
5. __________
6. __________
7. __________
8. __________
9. __________
10. __________
11. __________
12. __________
13. __________
14. __________
15. __________

*Adapted with permission from Claudia Black, *It Will Never Happen to Me* (Denver: ACT, 1982), p. 126.

SESSION 5
Making Better Decisions

OBJECTIVES:

To enhance your ability to make better decisions about how to take care of yourself in relationships.
To learn what a better relationship is.
To identify something you want to change in yourself.

I. OPENING THE SESSION

Review of Session 4: Ask members if they made progress in changing old role patterns:

The Overly Responsible One. Have you attempted to let go of a responsibility you do not need to assume or let someone else assume some responsibility? What thoughts and beliefs about yourself do you need to work on and change to do this more often?

The Caretaker/Rescuer. Have you paid attention to ways in which you attempt to rescue or become a caretaker this week? Did you notice how people react to you when you assume this role? How did you feel about yourself as you observed yourself assuming this role? What can you do to prevent rescuing and caretaking when it is not really needed or wanted?

The Superadaptable One. Did you attempt to make your own needs and desires more visible this week? Does anyone have any examples of self-assertion to report?

Fun Activity. How many of you treated yourself to some fun and let the child in you out to play this week? What were some of the fun things you did?

Ask members if they have any other progress to report regarding their attempts to free themselves from love addiction. Review the

Actor/Reactor Exercise (Exercise 8, Session 4). Ask members if they attempted to become more of an actor in expressing their own feelings, needs, and desires. Ask group if they experienced any insights as a result.

Review new messages for the three roles.

Overresponsible

- I can feel good about myself without being overresponsible.
- I don't have to be so responsible and serious all the time.
- It's O.K. to have fun.
- Everything doesn't have to be done my way. I can accept how others handle things.

Caretaker/Rescuer

- I ask others if they would like my help.
- I take care of myself.
- I cultivate other interests and ways to feel good.

Superadaptor

- I'm sensitive to my own needs, interests, and preferences.
- I can make my own decisions and choices based on what's important to me.

II. RELATIONSHIP EVALUATION INVENTORIES

It isn't easy to decide what action to take to best help yourself. One way to begin is by evaluating aspects of your relationships and considering how you think and feel about them. The following inventories are designed to help you obtain a more comprehensive view of your relationships.

A. Exercise One: Pleasurable Events Inventory

1. List events and activities that you particularly enjoyed during the past six months.
2. After each event or activity, indicate whether you did it with or without your partner by writing a P (with partner) or W (without partner).
3. Distribute "Relationship Satisfaction Inventory" handout and instruct members to complete.

B. Discussion

The purpose of these inventories is to increase your awareness and understanding of problem areas, not to immediately tell you how you are going to solve problems. We must learn what a healthy relationship is before we can discuss ways to develop healthy relationships.

Ask group to break into dyads and discuss the following: From completing these inventories, what have you learned about your level of satisfaction with your relationship?

- If you were to balance your relationships on a scale, which direction do your feelings about your relationships tilt? Toward satisfaction or dissatisfaction?
- Looking at the two inventories, what about your relationships pleases you the most and what are you most unhappy about?

III. WHAT IS A HEALTHY RELATIONSHIP?[1]

What's a healthy relationship? What does it look like/feel like? How do I develop one? How do I know if I have one?

In a healthy intimate relationship, the couple create an environment in which both individuals can express the following:

- I can be me.
- You can be you.
- We can be us.
- I can grow.
- You can grow.
- We can grow together.

A. I Can Be Me

State the following and ask members to provide other examples.

- A healthy relationship frees me to be myself.
- Your partner doesn't judge you. He allows and encourages you to develop yourself as a person.

How can you tell when you're being judged and feel inhibited from developing yourself as a person?

- When you're always afraid of making a mistake.
- When you always feel as if you're tiptoeing on eggshells.

Can you think of other ways?

B. You Can Be You

- In a healthy relationship, you give your partner the same freedom you want for yourself.
- You accept your partner as he is and don't try to change him. (Note: this doesn't mean you must accept undesirable and unhealthy qualities in your partner. Rather, you accept your partner as a whole person with strengths, limitations, and the ability to make positive changes in his life.)

C. We Can Be Us

- We are a couple with common likes, dislikes, and goals.
- We have differences, some unimportant and easy to work through, others more difficult to resolve. For example, "I hate pancakes" or "You always leave dirty dishes on the table" are problems that are relatively easy to resolve. But "I don't want children" or "I don't want to see your parents again" are complicated problems that will test the strength and commitment of your relationship.

D. I Can Grow

- My partner supports me in my efforts to grow as a person.
- My partner encourages me to be myself.

E. You Can Grow

- Your partner feels supported and encouraged by you.

F. We Can Grow Together

- We work together on goals we share.
- Our relationship grows as we grow individually.
- Our relationship is flexible enough to allow for change.

G. Intimacy

Intimate relationships are marked by warm friendship developed through long association. In intimate relationships, both individuals give and receive:

- Validation
- Understanding

- Value and respect intellectually, emotionally, and physically

The degree of intimacy is determined by the degree of sharing between two individuals.

H. A Healthy Relationship Is Not

- A power struggle (you don't have to think/feel the same about everything)
- Symbiotic or fused, wherein neither individual has an identity outside the other person
- Limited to a sexual relationship, but rather enjoys the pleasure of sharing and exploring life together

I. Ask group members what they can do that will let them experience a more positive and healthy relationship.

- Listen to each other.
- Assert your own needs, feelings, and desires.
- Express differences of opinions rationally.
- Develop your own talents, interests, independent activities, and friends.
- Respect your and your partner's need for privacy and space.
- Develop interests and activities to do as a couple.

J. I Can Be Me; You Can Be You; We Can Be Us

In healthy relationships, both individuals are able to establish separate interests and relationships. They aren't possessive or jealous of each other's time and interests, because each individual has interests of his or her own. They like themselves and feel their worth as individuals. They are able to express themselves and socialize both individually and as a couple. They communicate openly and trust the other, despite their differences in interests and opinion. Together, they are able to resolve differences, be they minor, such as who is more orderly than the other, or more serious, such as how much money is spent or how the children should be raised. They are able to communicate and negotiate their differences. They remain flexible and are able to adapt to and facilitate the needs of the other.

K. Exercise Two
1. Distribute "Signs of Healthy Love" handout.
2. Instruct members to complete, then discuss as a group.
3. Ask members to provide other examples.

L. Exercise Three
1. Distribute "Characteristics of Healthy Love and Addicted Love" handout.
2. Ask members to identify characteristics they need to work on.
3. Discuss as a group.

M. Exercise Four—Visualization
1. Close your eyes. Imagine yourself involved in a healthy intimate relationship in which you feel that, as we discussed earlier, "I can be me, you can be you, we can be us." The relationship can be with your present partner, with someone you know, or with someone you never met. The two of you are in a pleasant, relaxing environment—the beach, a quiet forest, a meadow filled with wildflowers, or perhaps you're sitting beside a waterfall or in front of a cozy fire in a comfortable room. Create your own special scene. (Pause.) Picture you and your companion as being happy enjoying the pleasant environment and being together.

   In this relationship you feel free to be yourself and your partner feels free to be him- or herself. You appreciate each other for your individual qualities, for both your differences and your similarities. (Pause.) Now picture the two of you joining together—perhaps talking together, sharing an interest, doing an activity, expressing affection. How do you feel both emotionally and physically? (Pause.) Picture the two of you growing, changing as individuals, and not feeling threatened. Imagine your relationship growing; you feel more fulfilled and have a clearer sense of self and your relationship as a couple. (Pause.) Meditate on this image for a while. (Allow two or three minutes of silence.)

2. As a group, discuss members' thoughts and feelings about this experience.

IV. MINI-LECTURE: MAKING BETTER DECISIONS[2]

The basic question regarding healthy relationships is not "Do I still love him?" but rather "Do I want to live with him every day?" "Does this relationship fulfill my needs?"

"Do I leave or do I stay?" Our thinking often gets stuck when we think we have only two choices: to stay or leave. When we formulate the problem in these terms, we tend to see one decision as all good and the other as all bad. Usually, we have more than two choices. We need to think in terms of various options.

One important option is to attempt to change yourself as opposed to changing or leaving the relationship. Instead of feeling stuck when you can't make a decision about your relationship, try considering your indecision as an opportunity. Consider your indecision, uncertainty, and ambivalence as an opportunity to take charge of your life—to explore new directions, to become more involved in what really matters to you. View your indecisiveness as an opportunity to get to know yourself better and to nurture your growing self. Think of it as a time for discovering your likes/dislikes, talents, wishes, and desires. Then pick and choose those activities and relationships that will promote your well-being and fulfillment.

If you leave the relationship, acknowledge this decision to yourself, even if you decide not to tell your partner right away. Don't use separation or divorce as a threat by saying, "I'm leaving unless you. . . ." Such tactics don't work in the long run, and you won't get the results you want.
Be patient. If you decide to leave, don't expect to solve all your problems at once. It's O.K. to take your time. You need time to think and work through problems and practical concerns, for example, finances, where to live, what it will be like living alone. Don't expect to clearly understand what you want; that's unrealistic. Don't force your decision by giving yourself deadlines. Most important, don't create an inci-

dent by starting a fight or having an open affair. To do so is to risk violence and tragedy. Even if your partner never hit you or even threatened you before, people sometimes act on impulse in the heat of emotional upset.

Think small. Continue to make little decisions and take tiny steps. Do one small thing for yourself each day. Get yourself out of your routine. Build your self-confidence. It takes practice and patience to build a well-balanced life that allows you to feel secure in yourself, regardless whether you leave or stay.

Some things you can do.

- Start a new activity.
- Get involved in something that interests you (view the activity as a survival technique that shakes you out of your routine).
- Look for activities that are rewarding physically, intellectually, creatively, and emotionally.
- Working women and mothers may need to slow down by practicing relaxation and meditation.
- Connect with other women through a friend or organization.
- Read women authors for information on how to develop new attitudes toward marriage and independence.
- Join or attend meetings of organizations that focus on women's issues.

Exercise Five

1. Ask group members to respond to the following questions:
   - What reactions, ideas, and thoughts of potential changes you want to make in your life were stimulated by today's session?
   - What small decisions and steps can you take to initiate changes in your life?
   - What can you do to connect more with other women?
2. Ask members to write their responses down.
3. Ask members to share their reactions/decisions with the group.

V. PREPARATION FOR THE FINAL SESSION

Ask members how we can make the final session helpful/meaningful. Are there specific topics they would like to talk about?

Ask members to think about what they hoped to learn or get from the group when the group first started. Compare what you have achieved with what you expected. How far have you progressed toward your goals? In next week's session, we will share how far we've progressed as well as plans we have for the future. We will also focus on staying unhooked.

VI. CLOSING

As group, do closing ritual.

References

1. Janet Woititz, *Struggle for Intimacy* (Pompano Beach, FL: Health Communications, Inc., 1985).
2. Lynette Triere, with Richard Peacock, *Learning to Leave: A Woman's Guide* (New York: Warner Books, 1982).

Handout—Session 5

Relationship Satisfaction Inventory*

This self-evaluation inventory can help you identify areas of satisfaction and dissatisfaction in your relationship. Rate each of the following aspects of your relationship from very high to very low satisfaction.

Very High **High** **Fair** **Low** **Very Low**

1. General emotional contentment ____________
2. Communication ____________
3. Companionship ____________
4. Sharing of interests ____________
5. Practical support ____________
6. Emotional support ____________
7. Growth support ____________
8. Feeling loved by my partner ____________
9. Feeling love toward my partner ____________
10. Feeling respected by my partner ____________
11. Feeling respect for my partner ____________
12. Feeling trusted by my partner ____________
13. Feeling trusting of my partner ____________
14. Feeling nurtured by my partner ____________
15. Feeling nurturing toward my partner ____________
16. Enjoyment ____________
17. Warmth ____________
18. Sexual satisfaction ____________
19. Feeling self-esteem in the relationship ____________
20. Wanting to spend time with my partner ____________
21. Shared values ____________

After completing these ratings, determine whether you have more areas of satisfaction or dissatisfaction in your relationship. Please note that the number of areas with which you experience satisfaction or dissatisfaction may not be as important as how crucial a particular area is for you. Are areas important to you not included in this inventory? Add them.

*Adapted with permission from Howard Halpern, *How to Break Your Addiction to a Person* (New York: McGraw-Hill, 1982), pp. 137–138.

Handout—Session 5

Signs of Healthy Love*

A fulfilling and mature love relationship has the following qualities. Mark with "I" if quality allows "I can be me"; with "Y" if it allows "You can be you"; with "U" if it allows "Us to be us."

A healthy relationship:

- Allows for individuality in both individuals _____
- Experiences both oneness with and separateness from one's partner _____
- Brings out the best qualities in both individuals _____
- Accepts endings _____
- Encourages openness to change and exploration _____
- Invites growth in the other _____
- Experiences true intimacy _____
- Allows for expression of needs and desires _____
- Experiences giving and receiving in the same way _____
- Does not attempt to change or control the other _____
- Encourages self-sufficiency of partners _____
- Accepts limitations of self and partners _____
- Does not crave unconditional love _____
- Finds commitment acceptable and desirable _____
- Develops high self-esteem _____
- Trusts the partner _____
- Appreciates solitude _____
- Expresses feelings spontaneously _____
- Welcomes closeness and risks vulnerability _____
- Cares with detachment _____
- Affirms equality of self and partner _____

*Adapted with permission from Brenda Schaeffer, *Signs of Healthy Love* (Minneapolis: Hazelden, 1986), pp. 3–4.

Handout—Session 5

Characteristics of Healthy Love and Addicted Love*

Healthy Love (Open System)	***Addicted Love (Closed System)***
Room to grow and express oneself; desires other to grow as well	Dependent; based on security and comfort; uses intensity of need and infatuation as proof of love (may really be fear, insecurity, loneliness)
Separate interests; outside friendships; maintains meaningful relationships outside relationship with partner	Total involvement; limited social life; neglects old friends and outside interests
Encourages personal development of the other; both individuals secure in their own worth	Preoccupation with other's behavior; dependent on other's approval for own identity and self-worth
Allows trust and openness	Jealous, possessive, fears competition
Mutual integrity preserved	One partner's needs are precluded by the needs of the other; self-deprivation
Willingness to risk and be real	Refuses to be vulnerable; eliminates risks
Explores feelings regarding relationship	Reassured through repeated, ritualized activity
Appreciates and enjoys solitude	Unable to endure separation (even in conflict); experiences withdrawal, loss of appetite, restlessness, lethargy, disorientation

Breakups

Accepts breakup without feeling a loss of adequacy and self-worth	Feels inadequate, worthless; a one-sided decision
Wants best for partner; can become friends	Violent ending; partners may hate each other; attempts to inflict pain; manipulates the other

*Adapted with permission from Melody Beattie, *Co-Dependent No More* (Minneapolis: Hazelden, 1987), pp. 101–102.

SESSION 6
Staying Unhooked

OBJECTIVES:

To identify important ways we can stay free of love addiction.
To celebrate our empowerment as individuals.
To evaluate the group experience.
To discuss the group members' interest in follow-up meetings or peer support.

I. OPENING THE SESSION

A. Review of Session 5: Ask members if they have questions or comments on previous week's session.

B. Brief overview of Session 6.

II. MINI-LECTURE: STAYING UNHOOKED

Addictive love is based on the belief that you *need* a relationship to be a whole person. Individuals who are vulnerable to addictive love are attracted to people who possess qualities that they lack in themselves. They look to another to provide them with what they feel is missing in themselves.

In reality, however, everyone has capabilities that have not been developed. As children we may not have developed our capabilities fully because we attempted to conform to others' expectations of us. Because of this, as adults we have limited knowledge of our own capabilities and feel that we lack something that only another person can provide. Such a belief leads to low self-esteem and an unhealthy dependency on partners.

Recovery begins when we reclaim our underdeveloped abilities and talents. To reconnect with disowned parts of yourself, you need to spend some time alone. Take time off from intimate relationships. This could mean a weekend or several months. You don't necessarily have to break off your relationship with your partner but tell him you need some time for yourself. As you get to know yourself better and begin reclaiming the missing pieces of yourself, you will begin to love yourself. You will feel less dependent on relationships. As a more whole person, you will attract and be attracted to other whole people. You will develop healthier relationships.[1]

To remain free of an addictive style of loving in your relationship, you need to work on the following three goals. Working toward these goals will also help you in deciding whether to stay in or leave a relationship, if that is an issue for you. If you decide to stay, working toward these goals will help you develop as an individual and consequently develop more healthy relationships with others. They will also help you in evaluating whether your current relationship can be salvaged to meet your newly defined needs and goals.

A. *Recognize and Release Thoughts and Feelings That Keep You Hooked to Unhealthy Relationships*
How many of you have or have had the following thoughts regarding the possible termination of a relationship?

- "I'll be lonely forever."
- "I'll never be loved again."
- "I'll never get over it."

Such fears have their roots in the helplessness and vulnerability of infancy and childhood. If your parents didn't come right away to feed you, change you, comfort you, or play with you, you experienced panic. Waiting, for an infant who's dependent on his or her parents for survival and love, feels like forever. The infant feels that his or her parents will never come, which leads to fears of abandonment. All infants have these experiences and fears. However, when we bring these feelings of helplessness and fear of abandonment into our adult life in addition to other negative experiences we had in our childhood, we're likely to relate to others in an addictive way. We may feel that we need a particular relationship in order to feel worthwhile and safe. One of the purposes of this workshop is to remind ourselves that for adults, dependent attachment to another person is harmful. Our partners and our friends aren't our only source of self-esteem; our interests, activities, and work can also make us feel good about ourselves.

B. *Recognize Self-defeating Thoughts That Keep You from Making Positive Changes in Your Life*
Monitor negative messages and self-criticism such as "I can't do that" or "I'll make a fool of myself." Talk back to your "internal critic": "No one expects me to do it perfectly. It's O.K. to make mistakes. I'm not a fool!" Do any of you criticize yourself in this way? Are you working to overcome it?

Use thought stoppage. When you become aware of a negative thought pattern, say, "STOP!" If appropriate, shout the word loudly or tell yourself silently. Substitute a pleasant scene or activity for the negative thought. Use the imaging techniques you have learned here. If the thought returns, repeat the process. Don't give up. Associate a pleasant thought or activity with stopping a negative thought.

C. *Develop Your Identity and Self-worth Independent of a Partner*
This goal is very important for achieving lasting changes in your life and relationships. Put your energies into developing yourself instead of always developing your partner. Once we begin to discover ourselves, perhaps for the first time, it becomes easier to let go of old fears from infancy and childhood. The more we develop our own identity, the better we understand ourselves and what we want. We begin to discover that we've outgrown our old roles and patterns of relating. We learn to credit ourselves for new skills and achievements. We're surprised by our new confidence. As we grow more independent, we discover that we no longer need someone to take care of us; we're quite capable, thank you, of doing this ourselves. We respect ourselves and feel secure knowing that we can truly depend on ourselves. We enjoy and value our time

alone. We take pride in our freedom from addiction in relationships.

You will stay unhooked if you commit yourself to continuing to grow as a person with the power to direct your own life. You will feel free to enjoy others as well as to seek help and accept it when you need it. Best of all, you will no longer need that addictive dependency on another person to feel good, happy, and fulfilled.

III. EXERCISES

A. Exercise One: Thoughts and Feelings

1. Break into dyads.
2. Tell your partner one of your self-defeating thoughts that keeps you hooked on love or keeps you from growing as a person. For example,
   - "I'll be lonely forever."
   - "I'll make a fool of myself."
   - "I can't do that."
3. Talk back to your internal critic or pessimist. Allow your partner to observe and provide feedback on your internal dialogue. Arrange your chairs so that your partner sits behind you. Your partner can play your alter ego by also talking back to your internal critic. You start first. Continue to "talk back." Part ners (alter ego) should "talk back" when they wish. If you can accept what your partner says, repeat it; if not, say, "I don't accept that."
4. Continue for approximately one minute, then reverse roles.
5. With your partner, discuss your reactions, and what you learned.
6. Reassemble as a group to discuss reactions and what participants have learned.

B. Exercise Two: Parenting Your Inner Child[2]

One way to help yourself stay unhooked and to keep from looking for someone to take of your needs is to begin filling your needs for yourself. You can do this by listening to your own "inner child" and talking to her.

That little child in you may be scared and in hiding. Make friends with her, nurture her, give her guidance.

Everyone has an inner child made up of all the thoughts and feelings we had as children. Our inner child affects us as adults in terms of how we react to everyday events. The inner child may be playful, creative, and curious about the world or may be fearful, insecure, and lacking self-esteem. Your inner child may still hunger for the love and attention she never received.

We also have within us inner parents based on childhood experiences of the loving parent and the punishing parent. You can counteract your overcritical and punishing inner parent by calling on your loving inner parent to nurture, reassure, and encourage your inner child.

Search out your inner child the next time you feel frightened or insecure. Often it's the inner child who is frightened. You can assume the role of the loving parent who gives your inner child the reassurance she needs. You, the adult, can then pursue your own goals, free from the fears of the inner child.

Close your eyes and imagine the little child in you. Perhaps she is sitting next to you, or perhaps you are holding her on your lap or cradled in your arms. Attend to this small child, who may be silent and frightened. Welcome her. Tell her that you will provide for her safety, take care of her, give her what she needs. Tell her that it's safe for her to grow up, to make her own decisions, to ask for what she wants, to say "NO." Let her know that it's O.K. to play and have fun, to decide whom she wants to spend time with and whom she doesn't want as a friend. Tell her it's all right to share her feelings. Let her know that you won't criticize her for being a baby. Tell her what you like about her. Let her know that she can always depend on you to be there for her, that you will listen, that you will give her your best guidance whenever she needs it, and that you will help her grow. Now, tell her how much you love her.

Visualize this scene for several minutes (three minutes). When you're ready, open your eyes.

What were your thoughts and feelings as you experienced this visualization?

C. Exercise Three: Reclaiming Your Whole Self[3]
In this exercise you will seek to reclaim parts of yourself that you may have devalued, discounted, disowned, or even left undiscovered.

As a child, perhaps you were not encouraged to be yourself. To please your parents, relatives, teachers, and other adults, you learned to hold a limited, myopic view of yourself. Maybe you quit trying to express yourself honestly and avoided exploring new interests or making new friends. When you quit developing and expanding your own individuality, you were left with a vague sense of incompleteness. As an adult you find yourself attracted to friends and romantic partners who possess those qualities you never developed in yourself. To feel whole, you look to others.

Look over the list of personal qualities in the handout and check those qualities that you find attractive in others. Add to the list if you wish.

With a partner, share one or two qualities that attract you most strongly and discuss how you might reclaim these qualities for yourself. (Allow 10 minutes.)

As a group, ask each participant to share one quality that she wishes to reclaim and what she will do to reclaim it for herself.

D. Exercise Four: Celebrating Your Empowerment
1. Using $8^{1}/2$ x 11 paper (or chart paper), make a draw-

ing—abstract or representational—that shows how you feel about your increased power and strength.

2. After you finish your drawing, look at it and think of one word or short phrase that describes your increased empowerment.
3. Moving around the group, have members show their drawing. Ask members to describe it briefly and to share their empowerment word or phrase.
4. Ask members to share their progress in achieving their goals since joining the group. Ask them to share their plans for ongoing progress and continued growth.
5. Tell members to applaud themselves.

IV. WORKSHOP EVALUATIONS

Ask members to provide written and verbal evaluations of the workshop.

V. ONGOING SUPPORT

Discuss the possibility of members forming a monthly group for continuing support and growth. If possible, the group leader may volunteer her services in helping them launch a peer-support group.

VI. CLOSING

References

1. Jody Hayes, *Smart Love* (Los Angeles: Jeremy P. Tarcher, 1989), pp. 78–80.
2. Brenda Schaeffer, *Is It Love or Is It Addiction* (Minneapolis: Hazelden, 1987).
3. Hayes, *Smart Love*, pp. 80–81.

Handout—Session 6

Personal Qualities

Sociable

Fun loving

Organized

Creative/imaginative

Intelligent

Attractive

Outgoing

Assertive

Ambitious

Athletic

Artistic

Independent

Self-confident

Optimistic